FORBIDDEN GATES

GOD'S TOUGH GUYS

Stephen, *the First Martyr*
Samuel Kirkland, *Missionary to the Senecas*
St. Vincent de Paul, *Priest and Pirate Captive*
Eric Liddell, *Olympic Star*

GOD'S TOUGH GUYS

FORBIDDEN GATES

A Story of Stephen, the First Martyr

DENISE WILLIAMSON

Illustrated by JOE BODDY

Wolgemuth & Hyatt, Publishers, Inc.
Brentwood, Tennessee

Wolgemuth & Hyatt, Publishers, Inc.
1749 Mallory Lane, Brentwood, Tennessee 37027

Book Development by March Media, Inc., Brentwood, Tennessee

First Edition September 1990

PRINTED IN THE UNITED STATES OF AMERICA

Library of Congress Cataloging-in-Publication Data

Williamson, Denise J., 1954-
　　Forbidden gates : a story of Stephen, the first martyr / Denise
Williamson : illustrated by Joe Boddy. — 1st ed.
　　　　p.　cm. — (God's tough guys)
　　Summary: After sneaking a Gentile friend through the forbidden
gates of the Temple, a young Jewish boy becomes a fugitive and meets
Stephen who teaches him how to be a real man for God.
　　ISBN 1-56121-026-9
　　1. Stephen, Saint. d. ca. 36—Juvenile fiction. [1. Stephen,
Saint, d. ca. 36—Fiction. 2. Saints—Fiction. 3. Fugitives from
justice—Fiction. 4. Christian life—Fiction.] I. Boddy, Joe,
ill. II. Title. III. Series: Williamson, Denise J., 1954-　God's
tough guys.
PZ7.W6714Fo　1990
[Fic]—dc20　　　　　　　　　　　　90-42911
　　　　　　　　　　　　　　　　　　　　　CIP
　　　　　　　　　　　　　　　　　　　　　AC

to
Mom and Dad

The LORD is my strength and my song;
he has become my salvation.

—Psalm 118:14

CONTENTS

1

THE CHALLENGE

An old man's coin hung in the balance.

Nathan watched his father squint toward the two round trays that dangled from the scales. After studying its weight, his father picked the coin off and handed it back to his frail customer.

"This coin has been trimmed," Nathan's father said. "It is too light. To purchase a temple coin, you must have another shekel."

The man's eyes narrowed. "But that's from my wages, sir," he said. "I've come to Jerusalem from Hebron. I must buy a sacrifice. It's the only coin I have."

Nathan's father ignored the wrinkles of despair around the traveler's gray lips. "Save your complaining for your employer," he advised. "If you don't have another coin, move on."

The man turned away, and a young woman took his place. She dropped a coin into the empty pan. "For the purchase of turtledoves," she said quietly. The hem of her blue shawl delicately covered her nose and mouth.

Nathan's father compared the tested temple weight, lying in one tray, with the woman's coin, placed in the other. The slightly swaying pans hung evenly. "A clean coin for you," he said as he pushed a drab Jewish token toward her. He threw her Roman piece into his money box. A hundred hammer-pressed images of handsome Roman officials looked out at Nathan before his father closed the lid. How Nathan liked the strong faces pictured on those coins, but it was a pleasure he kept to himself. Jewish law prevented faithful men from making images of any human being or animal. Only the Holy One himself, blessed be his name, had the right to give form to life, and only he deserved admiration and praise.

Still Nathan felt the excitement of guarding money from the most powerful government in the world. Just then his father touched his arm. "Son, watch the coin box and the scales for a while. I must walk through the portico to check some of the weights used by the bird-market vendors. I'll be back soon."

When Benjamin bar Azmon stood, his summer robe of ruby-colored silk whispered against the edges of the booth. He paused for a moment, looking down at Nathan with eyes as warm as the early afternoon sun. "How I rejoice to see you working at my own table for the first time," he said with a laugh. "Just yesterday, it seems, you were a little boy."

Nathan smiled back, sitting taller on the hard stool. "It's exciting to be on this side of a money-changer's table, Father. I think I'll like this work." He watched his father push through the crowds that flowed toward the Temple's inner gates.

As an amarkal, a temple trustee, Nathan's father held one of the most important posts in Israel. More than one head in the crowds turned as the tall banker moved from booth to booth. Today for the first time, on the fifth of Sivan, Nathan was actually here as his father's assistant. He would learn to judge an honest coin exchange and how to sell the temple sacrifices. Then, if he proved to be good enough at figures and earned the respect of the older temple leaders, he might someday take over his father's position.

The thought of it made Nathan's hand perspire against the metal balance. Could he, Nathan bar Benjamin, see *himself* as the richly dressed center of attention in this ogling crowd? As he considered his future, a boy perhaps no older than his own twelve years approached him. The boy's brow was wet with sweat. The leather band drawn across his forehead bore the weight of an enormous load of crates and baskets which lay against his back and shoulders. Nathan's own neck muscles tightened as the youth sagged under the burden larger than his own body.

"These are the bird baskets and crates you ordered," the boy said breathlessly. "Where should I unload them?"

In all his years Nathan had never gotten used to seeing such porters—these pathetic human substitutes for donkeys—plodding through the narrow streets. Talking with one so bent from the brutal work was more than he had prepared himself for on his first day in the marketplace.

The boy's load shifted and the head strap cut deeper into his sun-scorched face. "You tell me where to unload this cargo now!" he demanded suddenly.

His curtness brought Nathan to attention. He rose so that the stinking porter would not miss seeing the scholar's pen case dangling from his belt. "I'm no seller of birds," Nathan replied indignantly. "Go speak to Baruk. Over there."

The overburdened boy plowed into the crowds. A moment later Nathan saw him emerge at Baruk's elbow. He dropped his load right at the merchant's feet, but Baruk kept trading birds for coins as fast as his chubby hands could move. The boy would not be ignored, and a heated exchange of words followed. Soon Baruk was storming toward Nathan's booth. Behind him he dragged the porter by one wrist. In his anger Baruk nearly toppled several of his own cages packed with live doves and pigeons.

"You, there!" the merchant called out to Nathan. "Get up and help this fool unload his goods for me!"

Nathan blinked in amazement at the absurd command.

"Can't you see?" Baruk raged. "It will take this boy half the day to stack his delivery. I can't have cages scattered everywhere like this! They're blocking customers!"

Nathan saw his father approaching Baruk from the rear. The temple official turned the merchant around with a firm hand.

Baruk, obviously embarrassed at being caught trying to press a trustee's son into service, tried hard to explain. "You see, Amarkal," he braved, "I ordered these crates long ago. Now, on the day before the Feast of Harvest, this stupid boy delivers them. His load is in the way of the crowds. It must be moved immediately."

Nathan's father folded his arms across his chest. "My son is not a laborer, Baruk."

Baruk grimaced and gave a little bow. "But the people are waiting to buy—"

"It cannot be helped," Nathan's father cut him off. "If that young man starts to work now, at least the job will be quickly begun."

Baruk grabbed the tired youth by his ear. The boy's eyes, flooding with pain, turned to Nathan. They were piercing eyes like those of the birds that bobbed their heads and watched from behind the wooden bars.

The boy twisted, but Baruk held him tightly. "You be quick!" Nathan heard the merchant say. "And if you ever deliver again during a major feast, I swear by the Temple itself, I'll never do business with your grandfather again."

Baruk finally set the boy free at the pile of crates. Then to Nathan's surprise the porter straightened himself and challenged the angry man so loudly that his words rang down from the porch roof. "We have no way of keeping track of your endless religious holidays," he shouted. "We make the best cages in the city. You take them when you get them, or *you* are the fool!"

A crowd gathered at the outburst, and Nathan moved closer to see what would happen next. Baruk was livid. "A fool!" he roared. He looked angrily at the spectators, then bent close to the boy. "What do you mean? *My* holidays?" he gasped. "I should have guessed it. You and your grandfather deceive me! You're not even Jews!"

"Of c-course, we're Jews!" the boy said hastily, his face now tense with worry. "Your holidays, merchant? By that, I only meant that for a poor laborer like myself nothing but work lies between Sabbaths. I am uneducated. How can I possibly count the days as you do?"

"A Jew knows his feast days," Baruk said bitterly. "I should speak to you in Hebrew now, not in this wretched Greek tongue of yours. Would you understand any of it?" He clinched his fists against his thighs. "Oh yes, this very moment I could prove you are not a Jew."

The boy swallowed hard. He looked at Nathan, but Nathan's father stepped forward and blocked the view.

"Place these crates correctly," Benjamin ordered. "See that Baruk gives you what he has agreed to pay you, and then leave the Temple Mount at once."

Baruk fumed. "I will purchase nothing from that family again. And I'll tell every Jewish vendor within a day's walk of Jerusalem to do the same."

Nathan's father turned to him. "Watch that hot-headed boy," he said. "He and Baruk have disgraced each other publicly. See that the youth doesn't vent his anger on the merchant's birds." Then his father left to soothe some of Baruk's impatient customers.

Reluctantly Nathan moved to the giant pillar built into the back wall of the portico. The hot grainy smell of caged birds was thick there. That odor, along with the thought of being caught again by the boy's sharp gaze, made his stomach roll.

When the youth carried the first stack of cages to the wall, Nathan noticed the sweat painting rivers down the boy's hollow cheeks. By the fourth load, he saw the tremors in the laborer's sinewy arms and legs. Thankfully the youth kept his eyes turned away. Nathan longed to do the same. Still his father had asked him to oversee so he was a captive observer of the boy's struggle. Nathan wondered how long it had been since he had eaten. Certainly he lived and breathed in poverty. His tunic proved it.

Suddenly the boy's dark eyes met his again. A moment later, the porter collapsed to the floor.

Nathan rushed to him. "You're ill," he said. "What should I do?"

The boy forced himself up to his knees. "I am sick with fatigue. That is all." He wiped a hand across his forehead. "A moment ago—you could have helped me. Why show kindness now?"

Nathan stepped back. "You heard my father's words. I was forbidden to do your work."

"Go away!"

"Not until I know that you can stand," Nathan replied.

The boy fell back against the cages. The startled birds sent feathers flying. His face crinkled into a tearful, exhausted laugh. "What's with you?" he asked with his head resting against one raised hand. "By not helping me, you hurt me. Now you boldly stand ready to heal. By the gods, you Jews are strange."

Nathan's head reeled from the pagan oath. It dawned on him that in his whole life he had not had *one* conversation with anyone outside the faith. If he had not been studying Greek to prepare for banking, he would have had no way of communicating with this heathen on the floor.

"*You* are the puzzle!" Nathan returned hotly. "You swear by all gods, yet make your living by pretending to serve one."

The boy stared at him from foot to head. "Look at your fine sandals—and the ring on your finger. Have you ever gone one day without bread?"

Nathan shook his head, feeling hot in his linen robe.

The boy closed his eyes. "I'll tell you something, though you won't understand it. I just destroyed my grandfather's business by one unguarded use of my angry tongue. When he finds out, he'll beat me. He'll turn me out. I will have nowhere to go."

Nathan studied him, unable to reply.

"When I leave here," the boy said, "I will never set foot on this Temple Mount again. Since I was a child coming here to sell my grandfather's handiwork, I have dreamed of sneaking into the Temple to see your God of the Four Horns. I have always wondered what such a creature looks like. . . ."

"There are four horns mounted on our *altar*—not on the One we serve," Nathan chided. "Human eyes can't look upon the Holy One, for we worship the Almighty God, Maker of Heaven and Earth."

The boy clenched his teeth. "Heaven and earth!" he scoffed. "If your god is the creator of all things, then he is my maker too. Yet you may visit him at this Temple, and I may not? Does such religion make sense to you?"

Nathan groped for a reply. "God chose to show his holiness among men by means of one nation, the Jewish people," he said finally.

The boy pointed a sagging finger toward Baruk's booth. "Jews show nothing of holiness!" he snorted.

"You should not have overstepped your boundaries," Nathan said, his sympathy waning. "The Almighty One has set the Jews apart from all nations to be holy as He is holy. Because of this we eat and work and trade among ourselves. You should not have tricked Baruk into thinking you were a Jew."

The boy sighed. "I knew it was impossible for you to understand. You have no idea what it's like to live in a country where only Roman soldiers and Jews think they have the right to breathe."

"Don't put my people and the Romans in the same breath," Nathan warned. "We hate their foreign rule.

Someday we believe the Almighty One will send a leader to set our people free."

The youth hung his head. "May we all be set free," he half whispered. Then he looked at Nathan with eyes growing bright. "If today I could see into this great Temple of yours, perhaps I would come to feel as you do. Then when your leader comes, I could leave my grandfather for good and put myself into his service."

"It's not that simple," Nathan told him. "No one in Palestine knows who this leader will be or when he will come. My people have been waiting for years, and it may be many more years before our savior—Messiah—comes. Worse for you, there is a law that keeps non-Jews from setting foot beyond the Soreg that guards the inner courts."

"Where is this Soreg?" the boy asked.

Nathan looked out toward the crowds. As he feared, his father had been watching him. "I must go," he said abruptly. "My father sees us talking."

The boy eyed him angrily. "You would let your father's opinion keep me from coming before this One True God you speak of?"

"I told you, it's not that easy." Nathan began to walk away. "As a Gentile you cannot pass through the forbidden gates."

"Where is this Soreg?" the boy demanded again.

Nathan pointed far across the open courtyard. "Way over there," he said. "See the fence built with lacy stonework? That's it, and if you could read, you'd find warnings posted in your own language. Step through any one of the openings in the Soreg—you die! My father and his friends will see to it."

The boy suddenly rose to his feet and followed Nathan. "If I offered something of value, could you find a way for me to go through?" he asked.

"Something of value—from you?" Nathan snorted. Instantly he hated himself for his reply. "Sorry," he said, "but what of val—?"

The boy had dug into a bag hanging around his neck. He pushed some hard objects into Nathan's hand.

Nathan took a quick look. Two beautifully carved turtledoves lay side by side on his palm. "Idols," he said almost to himself, but he did not drop them.

"They are not idols," the boy protested. "These are things I carve myself. Sometimes I sell them in the upper marketplace by Herod's Palace." He paused. "You can keep them . . . if you get me inside that Temple. I have fixed my mind on it. I want to go."

Nathan looked into the boy's excited face. "You could be killed!"

"With my grandfather's anger I may be dead already," he replied. "Take me to see the place of your God."

"Tell me your name," Nathan said.

"Dorian."

Nathan trembled as his hand closed around the perfectly matched birds. "All right, Dorian," he said. "Follow the porches around to the right. You will see a wide ramp leading up from the stables on the lower level. If I decide to help you, I'll meet you there soon."

2

BREAKING THE LAW

Within the hour Nathan found Dorian sitting against the wall, his knees drawn up to his chest, his hair hiding his face and spreading out almost to the tips of his thin elbows. Nathan was glad he had taken time to go home for an extra robe in which to hide Dorian. In his present dress, he would not pass for even the poorest of Jews traveling to Jerusalem for the Feast of Harvest.

Slipping to Dorian's side, Nathan sat down on the cool stone floor. "Don't look up," he warned. "Not until I leave."

Dorian had chosen a good meeting place, one made private by the flowing, ever-changing sea of cloaks that rippled near them as men and women surveyed the vendors' booths. The shoppers were intent on the displays of grain and fruits and souvenir trinkets from the holy city—not on two boys resting against the wall. Nathan watched so that no one would see him press the fine robe he carried against Dorian's bare leg. Then he pushed an expensive woven cap onto the Gentile's head.

"I will go to the pillar directly in front of us and wait for you," Nathan told him quietly. "Slip on my robe, and meet me there. But say nothing to me. Keep two steps from me as we pass through the gate and while we are inside. When we get back through the Soreg, come directly here to shed my robe."

Nathan paused, half hoping Dorian would decide against the plan. But the boy was as unresponsive as a merchant napping beside his wares. His heart pounding, Nathan walked to the pillar. Almost immediately Dorian drew near. He had wrapped the robe around himself. It covered him well enough.

Nathan went directly to the Soreg. He passed through the nearest gate without hesitation, though his eyes fell upon the warning signs posted beside it. They were written in Hebrew, Latin, and Greek. Every language bore the same information:

A non-Jew brings on his own sudden death by trespassing beyond this barrier.

How many times Nathan had read those signs before and used them as practice boards for comparing the three languages he studied. Now he was helping one foolhardy heathen to break the law. For a moment Dorian's birds, tucked in the hem of Nathan's sleeve, did seem like idols. Was he putting himself against God in this endeavor? The question stopped him in his tracks, and Dorian moved two steps ahead of him.

The imbecile! Nathan raged silently. Hadn't the boy

understood? He would lead. He marched past Dorian and climbed the white marble steps to the first high silver-and-gold-covered gate.

"The Court of Women," Nathan whispered as they went through the deeply shadowed opening in the temple wall.

Immediately Dorian's attention was drawn to the west, as Nathan knew it would be. Far across the inner courtyard, the magnificent columns of Nicanor's Gate gleamed gold and white against the clear afternoon sky.

"This is too much for words," Dorian breathed. "Will we walk even over there?"

"Keep quiet," Nathan scolded. Yet he admired the poor boy's eye for beauty. They crossed the courtyard, which buzzed with the conversations of men and women, and slowly climbed the fifteen semicircular steps that spread down from Nicanor's Gate like a flowing white robe.

Dorian was craning his neck to get a good look at the wonderfully formed acanthus leaves capping the four Corinthian columns. Of course a boy with his artistic abilities would be impressed, Nathan mused. Despite the danger, he found himself enjoying his position as guide. Since the period of afternoon prayer was close to starting, the court was becoming more crowded. The increase in activity gave Nathan a sense of security, though he knew he had to be careful because many familiar faces—including his father's—might appear in the crowds.

When the boys reached the landing, Nathan

touched the stone column nearest them. Dorian did the same, and they exchanged quick grins. Nathan could not resist speaking to him. "Directly through the gate is the Court of Israel," he said, "just underneath those narrow porches. Beyond that, where the altar rises, is the Court of Priests."

"Let's go in," Dorian urged. "Your priests weave and bow like gods floating in the mists of morning. It's terrible to watch them from so far away."

Nathan felt his eyes grow wide. Dorian had no understanding of what he suggested. "Only ceremonially clean men go in there," Nathan explained. "Tomorrow marks my thirteenth birthday, and I will be allowed to join the men for the first time. I will carry special loaves of bread to the priests as my thank offering."

"Well, I am going in *now*," Dorian announced, and before Nathan could grab him, he pushed past the other spectators.

Nathan held his breath as Dorian bobbed through the lines of Jewish men who stood praying or waiting with sacrifices. Moment by moment he saw his own cap moving within the congregation, but then it disappeared. All at once Nathan saw the Gentile again. He was stepping across the priests' court to touch the altar of the Lord!

Nathan rushed in. Dorian had the power to defile this holy place. Dodging this way and that, Nathan weaved a narrow pathway through the worshipping men. Finally he got a hand on Dorian's wrist. "You fool! Get back!" he whispered.

"Wait!" Dorian pleaded, his gaze fixed upward on the priests ascending the altar ramp. "Let me stand here for a moment. This is a wonderful celebration for an Unseen God."

"You fool!" Nathan raged again. He jerked Dorian's thin body back into the crowds. He dragged him to the back wall, in the shadow of the portico covering the Court of Israel.

"I'm leaving!" Nathan huffed. "In a moment the guards will find you and pick your bones."

Already loud murmurs were moving through the crowd as men talked about what they had just seen at the altar. Hiding his face with his hands, Nathan tried to slip away. Frantically he pushed toward Nicanor's Gate. He had to get there before someone in the crowd linked him with the other boy.

Two burly Levite guards rushed at Nathan. He ducked, and their shoulders brushed his own as they hurried past him to grab the heathen. Nathan made another try for the outer court. But because of the guards, hundreds of angry, excited onlookers were gathering to watch. They cut him off from the exit as completely as a wall. There was no moving now. He was forced either to turn back to Dorian or face the thousand questioning eyes that stared toward the Gentile.

The press of the crowd pushed him closer to the boy. Soon Nathan found himself only an arm's length away from Dorian.

"I don't believe that robe and cap belong to you," one of the thick guards growled. He loosed his hold on

Dorian for a moment while he stripped the boy to his own shabby clothes.

"These garments are much too fine for a dog," the other guard agreed, taking the robe and rolling it under his arm. "We'll soon know which Jew you stole them from."

Dorian glared at them like a silent, cornered animal.

"Humph!" one guard told the other. "I don't even think the swine speaks our language. Look at him." He stroked his beard, his face breaking into a spiteful grin. *"You are a dog,"* he said, this time in Greek.

Dorian screamed. "I am no dog!" He kicked at the Jew's shins.

"No, you're right," the guard went on in Greek, his face reddening. "You are nothing more than a heathen swine! Your very presence makes this place unclean! Don't you know you seek death by being here?"

"I seek God, the Maker of Heaven and Earth," Dorian braved.

"You are not worthy to say his name!" another Levite snapped. He pulled Dorian's wrists forward so they could be bound with rope.

"If a Creator made me, I have the right to know him," Dorian said steadily. His eyes searched the crowds.

Nathan, in a panic, turned his back. Using his outstretched hands like a knife, he cut between two elderly men. He kept squeezing through the spectators, and finally he bolted through Nicanor's Gate.

On the bright unroofed plaza outside, children skipped around their mothers' skirts. Men talked in clusters. But Nathan's heart was missing beats. He pushed into the fringes of a group in hopes of hiding from the guards.

The men he had joined were arguing among themselves. He had no interest in the discussion bouncing back and forth between speakers though he did make sure he was out of sight from the three Sadducees who were his father's friends. These temple leaders were hotly challenging a large group of Greek-speaking Jews. They had probably come to Jerusalem for tomorrow's celebration. Nathan edged toward them. The guards, he reasoned, were less likely to sort him out from this crowd of strangers. He put himself behind the wide shoulders of a white-haired Jew in such a way that he could keep one eye on Nicanor's Gate.

Soon the burly Levites he had seen inside descended into the women's court. The men around Nathan noticed the guards' approach. Like sheep catching sight of wolves, they became wary and alert.

"Look, they're leading away a boy," some child called out as Dorian's thin frame became visible to the crowds. Behind the guards, curious men from the Court of Israel were coming out. Whispers spread across the court like an invisible flood. People started pushing in the direction of the guards. Some were shouting, "Away with the trespasser! Do away with the trespasser!"

Nathan moved to the edge of the courtyard to avoid

being swept along with the flow. Suddenly he was being called by name. His father and his Uncle Asher, a temple chief priest, rushed toward him. "What's happening?" his father asked.

Nathan tensed. "How should I know? I was just here for afternoon prayer, as I told you I would be."

Asher nodded. "Looks like they caught a Gentile trespassing in the Court of Israel." He surveyed the noisy crowd. "Come on. The guards seem to be having a hard time making their way out through the gates. Let's see if we can be of help."

Nathan's feet melted into the stone pavement.

"Come along," his father said. "You're going to face many such problems as a temple leader. It will be good for you to see what happens."

Nathan gritted his teeth and followed like a reluctant shadow. The amarkal pushed his way into the thick of the conflict. The crowds were shuffling nervously. A youthful man, his face with sharp features not unlike those so often copied on pagan statues and coins, stood confronting the Levites.

"So, you're a Greek-speaker, too," one guard rasped. "I hope, for your sake, that this heathen is not your son."

"I am a Jew," the man replied. "I have never laid eyes on the boy before. Still I beg for mercy for him."

Nathan recognized him. He was one of the foreigners who had been debating with the temple leaders.

"Move along!" the guard ordered. "If it were not

the eve of the feast, he would be tried today. As it is, the leaders will have to decide what to do with him until after the Sabbath."

"Yes," the man said, now speaking Hebrew. "I know the temple rules. And that is exactly why I voice my concern. The boy may not have a fair trial in a council full of Sadducees and priests who do what they can to please Rome."

With lightning speed the guard threw his open hand within a finger's width of the man's high cheekbone. "You watch your mouth, you Greek! It speaks against those in the House of the Lord."

Despite the threat, the man did not shrink back. He looked at Dorian with kindness. "Where is your family?" he asked in the youth's own tongue. Dorian opened his mouth, but he had no chance to reply. The guards formed a living fence around him so that he was completely cut off.

"If you want to speak for this prisoner," a guard snapped, "be at the council on the first day of the week. If you want to talk with the boy himself, I suggest you check later—with the Roman guards at the Antonia."

Then they forced Dorian away. The tall man who had tried to help stood looking after him.

Asher and Nathan's father walked Nathan to the next set of steps outside the gate of the women's court so they would not lose sight of the prisoner. Silently Nathan watched the Levites take Dorian down the last steps and shove him through an opening in the Soreg. There he

was handed over to two Roman soldiers who had been patrolling the Gentile court.

"They'll hold him at the Antonia until we Jews decide his fate," Asher told Nathan.

Nathan turned to walk away from the painful sight, but his father called him back. "Look at that boy one more time. Isn't he the one who was causing trouble for Baruk?"

"He's so far away, who could tell?" Nathan snapped, as the soldiers dragged Dorian across the Court of the Gentiles and up the steps of the Roman fortress, which overshadowed the northwest corner of the Temple Mount. Nathan started trembling. He could not tell if this gripping fear was for Dorian or for himself.

His father eyed the visitors still pouring in toward the Temple from the north and west gates. "Something must be done to stop them," he said to Asher. "If that Gentile's been on holy ground, the Temple must be closed and cleansed."

"On the eve of the Feast of Harvest? With this crowd?" Asher gasped. "It would set off a riot in Jerusalem. The idea is absurd."

Nathan's father glared back. "It is impossible to carry on worship if the Temple has been defiled," he countered. He looked beyond Asher to the cluster of religious officers who were running down the steps toward them.

"Please come inside, Amarkal," one of the gray-haired men begged. "You too, Asher. We must decide what to do. We've been talking with witnesses, and from what we've heard, there were *two* boys at the altar. If we don't close the gates immediately, that second one might get away."

3

CAUGHT!

As soon as his father and his uncle returned to the inner courts, Nathan raced through the streets to his home in the Upper City. He entered by the gate in the garden wall. No servant was in sight so he went to his second-story bedchamber by way of the outer stairs. Once inside he felt safer, but far from calm. He stood in the middle of the room, not knowing how to shake off his fear.

He could not stop thinking of Dorian. Finally he left the house and climbed another flight of stairs to the rooftop. The flat walled area was, after sunsets, their coolest room. From here, Nathan could look across the city to the Antonia, erupting like a man-made mountain from the gray skyline of roofs. Nathan knew some cell in that monstrous structure held Dorian prisoner. But with the very next breath, he made himself forget. *Why should I care?* He blew out his lungs. *Why should I care at all?*

He pulled Dorian's birds from his sleeve. The gold sunlight showed the exquisite details that he had not seen in the dim marketplace. He held the carvings toward the sky and stared at them for a while. Then in a sudden frenzy, he hurled the birds into the street below. *I am Esau*, Nathan thought bitterly. *I have traded my birthright for a treasure that could not last.* He dropped to the bench beside him in a fit of remorse. The sound of familiar footsteps drew his mind back home. Old Bena, his nursemaid, was coming.

She placed a hand on his shoulder. "Tired from your first day of work in the Temple?" she asked. He shrugged as he saw the twinkle in her eyes. "Even so," she continued, "you'd better start your evening preparations, young master. Must I remind you of the importance of this night?"

Wearily he shook his head. Though he loved her like a mother, he wished she'd go away.

Bena gazed at him. "Here is a boy with a troubled heart," she pronounced.

He straightened, realizing that he must hide his thoughts. "It's the feast," he replied. "I'm concerned that I will not respond as a man should. I feel so much like a boy." He was not lying. This would have been his only worry, if it had not been for Dorian.

"You will do well," she assured him. "You are the apple of your father's eye. You would have been your mother's joy, if she had lived to see this night."

Nathan wanted to cry against her shoulder and tell her the whole truth, but he sat motionless. Tonight, on the first Sabbath of his thirteenth year, he would put aside all childish ways.

"I have drawn your bathwater, and your clothes have been laid out," Bena said. Tears welled in her eyes. "Forgive me," she sniffed, "but you are like a son to me, Nathan bar Benjamin. And after today, Shem will attend you, since it is no good for an old woman to be a young man's servant."

Again, Nathan longed to embrace her, but he did not. When she left the rooftop, he realized he had never felt so alone. He forced himself to go inside. In the tiled bathroom he washed and dressed in the elegant garments that had been prepared for him. For weeks he had been wondering what wonderful surprises his father would lavish upon him. Since his birthday fell on the sixth day of Sivan, the Feast of Harvest, nothing would be spared in making it a festive extravaganza.

But because of his foolishness, the beautiful clothes gave him no satisfaction, and the thought of tomorrow's feast was a burden. The thing he had desired most—to be counted as a man in the congregation of Israel—was now the thing he dreaded. Tomorrow he would dance and sing the sacred five-psalm Hallel before the altar with Israel's men. He shuddered. *Certainly he would be recognized there as the one who had been with Dorian.*

He plodded down the inside stairway, and his father greeted him. "Shalom, my son. We will dine here in the front room this evening. I have closed off the upstairs banquet room so that you will not see its decorations until tomorrow."

Nathan made himself sound happy. "What a wonderful surprise. As with these beautiful garments, Father, I am not worthy of these things."

"Nonsense!" his father exclaimed. "You are my only son, my only heir. I have waited since you were born to see this day. Tomorrow you come to the Temple as a man." He took Nathan's hand and removed the simple gold ring that had been on his finger since he was six. He replaced it with one set with black onyx and ruby stones.

"Father!" Nathan gasped. "It's beautiful! I don't know what to say."

His father laughed. "I'm glad you like it. Now come to dinner. Your Uncle Asher is at the table."

A servant went ahead of them to draw back the curtain. The table now exposed was spread with an astonishing variety of meats and summer fruits. Asher rose from the dining couch to greet them.

"Shalom, Nathan. I am delighted your father has allowed me to join you." They washed their hands in the bowl by the wall. When Nathan finished, both men motioned for him to occupy the middle couch, the traditional seat of honor.

"Oh, I couldn't, I shouldn't—" Nathan protested.

"Take it," his father said. "Tonight begins your celebration." Almost with the same breath, his father raised his voice and prayed aloud in the dim glow of the sabbath lamp he lighted.

Timidly Nathan stretched across the couch, his weight resting on his left elbow, his right hand remaining free. His father served him first, giving him only the finest morsels from each bowl. They stopped passing food for a moment as his father recited another prayer.

Nathan ate in silence, his stomach aching with every thought of Dorian in prison.

Asher, however, seemed anxious to speak. "Well, how about this afternoon?" he said eagerly. "I, for one, am glad that the Sanhedrin is forbidden to convene on the eve of a feast. I think we did quite well at reaching a decision on the trespass case without getting the whole seventy-man legal council involved."

"How can you say that?" Nathan's father pointed a finger at his brother. "It's hard for me to believe what I saw and heard today. Only a handful of leaders even brought up the sacred law when we talked about the possible defilement of the altar. The rest of the men had one thing on their minds—that the Temple be kept open regardless of what took place inside. . . ."

"You should be happy, Amarkal," Asher said with a nod. "These men are good businessmen. They know what would happen in Jerusalem if the Temple were closed for a festival."

Nathan's father angrily wiped his fingers. "Is this a marketplace we run—or the House of God?"

Asher savored a bite of roast from his dish. "Haah, Benjamin," he teased. "If you really want to get to the bottom of this, I think you should go after that Stephen fellow who was hindering the guards. I wouldn't be surprised if *he* put the boy up to going right in through the Soreg and Nicanor's Gate. You know what he thinks of the Temple."

Benjamin nodded. "He used to be quite a burr in our tail, that's true, debating the scholars and questioning how this Temple could be holy when so much of it is built with Roman money. He's a smart, Greek-trained, synagogue Jew. I would suspect him, but we hadn't heard from him in quite awhile."

"That's because he joined up with those followers of The Way," Asher reminded him, "and you know they're not saying much now that their leader's dead."

"I see them coming to the Temple for prayer," Benjamin observed as he put some dried fruit on his brother's plate.

Asher munched on the raisins. "Probably begging the Almighty One's forgiveness for calling a simple Galilean carpenter the 'King of the Jews.'" He smirked.

"Father, you know some people don't believe that this man is dead," Nathan put in, thinking of the mysterious ghost stories that kept blowing through the marketplace.

His father frowned. "I want you to be open with your questions about the tales you've heard, Nathan. At the same time, I want you to start guarding your ears and your heart—these rumors aren't for faithful Jews."

Nathan nodded obediently, wondering if his father would consider this to be a firm promise. During their daily scripture studies with the temple instructors, Nathan and the other young scholars often wandered off on discussions about the coming Messiah's work and reign. Sometimes they'd even talk about this dead Jesus of

Nazareth, trying to compare what they knew of his life with the prophecies in the Scriptures. To Nathan, this puzzling over past and future events was so much more exciting than memorizing line after line of written law.

"I guess you heard the latest rumor," Asher said, bowing over his plate. "Recently, it's been said, Jesus was seen disappearing from the Mount of Olives *in a cloud.* Quite convenient, I'd say, since this will explain why no one can see him anymore! Haah!" He rested his head on his hand. "It's sad how quickly the ignorant turn to superstition, isn't it?"

"It's not just the unlearned," Benjamin said as he poured tall clear glasses of wine. "You'd think by now every Jew in Jerusalem would know this man was no Messiah." He motioned for a break in the conversation so he could speak the after-meal benediction.

Asher took his glass. "I've never seen it worse. Usually followers disband when their leader dies, but it must be more than twenty days since the Romans nailed Jesus to a cross. Twenty days—and still his name is on many lips."

Nathan's father corrected him. "More than forty days, Brother. It was Passover when he was arrested. Don't you remember? I do, because Nicodemus the Pharisee and one or two other temple leaders made themselves ceremonially unclean for the feast by helping with the man's burial. That I will long remember, but never understand."

"I think such actions just show the restlessness our

people face in the midst of this hateful Roman rule. Discouraged as they are, even leaders can start to grab at silly dreams."

Benjamin looked at his brother. "If only our suffering would create a deeper longing for the One True God," he mused.

The two men sat silently for a while. Finally Asher raised his glass. "The best of wines," he said.

Nathan could not bear the lull. "What's going to happen to the boy who was caught today?" he blurted out.

Asher looked him in the eye. "Who cares?" he shrugged.

Nathan drew in his breath. It was dangerous to press the matter.

His uncle's face softened. "But I'll tell you anyway since I pride myself in having much to do with the arrangements that have been made."

Nathan played with an almond in its shell. He tried to appear only half-intersted in what Asher had to say.

"I've worked it out so that the Romans will have to keep that young man and decide his fate themselves," Asher boasted.

"What?" Nathan's father roared. "If that boy's guilty of trespass, he deserves to die. Roman law still gives us the right to execute him ourselves—and this should happen as soon as the Sanhedrin decides his case."

Asher tipped his head. "It's so much better to let Rome deal with this. Can't you understand? Putting a young boy to death would make us look bad in the eyes of Jerusalem's population."

"I can't believe you, Asher," Nathan's father sighed. "We're responsible for doing what is right according to the law, not according to the whims of popularity."

"The boy's Roman punishment will surely be enough. You see, I presented the stolen robe and cap he wore as evidence that the boy is a thief. As far as I know, no family has come to speak for him. So, you know what that means. . . ."

"That he'll go to the cross!" Nathan stammered in horror. "Romans kill thieves! The guards will drive nails through his hands and—"

"Nathan, Nathan," his father said, leaning toward him with an arm on the table. "Why are you in such a state? I doubt that crucifixion will come to a boy who steals from Jews. Rome is not so protective of our property."

"Your father's probably right," Asher said with a sharp glance at Nathan. "More likely he will be sold as a slave. The money Rome earns from the sale of his person will cover the expenses of holding him in prison. So it will work out fine. The Sanhedrin will not have to put anyone to death, and the heathen will be out of our way forever."

Benjamin sighed. "I still don't like it. Perhaps the temple leaders will be less softhearted if and when they find that second boy."

Nathan's heart started hammering his chest. His

father looked at him with concern. "You know, we almost ruined this meal with unhappy conversation," he reflected. "Come, let's go to the roof and relax. After all, the Sabbath is for our enjoyment—not our worry." He poured Asher more wine. "Brother, would you like to join me? Nathan, you may come too."

"Of course," Asher said. "But before we go, I'd like a private word with my nephew here."

"Certainly," Benjamin said. "Come up when you're ready."

Asher waited until Nathan's father left the room, then leaned close to Nathan. "The robe, the cap—" he whispered. "I recognized them. They are yours!"

Nathan's tightly held emotions exploded. "No!" he shouted. "That's not true!"

Asher squeezed his arm. "You were seen," he said. "There are witnesses who saw you with the boy in the marketplace, at the Soreg, and in the Court of Priests! But you should be grateful—no one has come up with your name *yet*. The most the Levites know now is that it was some young, wealthy Jew." Asher's fingers bit into his flesh. "Your stupid prank will ruin both your father and me—you know that—unless I can keep the Sanhedrin from tracing the deed to you."

"I never meant to hurt Father," Nathan gasped. "I never wanted to—"

"It's too late for regret," Asher scolded. "We must have a plan."

"Do anything!" Nathan begged. "Do anything to keep us from being shamed."

Asher grabbed hold of Nathan's chin. "I think I know a way. But you must pay a price for my help."

"Anything. I'll do anything," Nathan choked.

His uncle sat back. "I thought you'd feel this way. That's why I've already mentioned to the temple leaders that you were not at prayer today. As long as the Gentile stays in Roman hands, I'm sure no one will come looking for you."

"Oh, thank you, thank you," Nathan cried. He scurried over to kiss his uncle's feet.

"None of this!" Asher stopped him. "But you must do me a favor."

Nathan blinked the tears from his eyes. "What?" he asked.

"Out in the garden, behind the jars that hold the washing water, there is a money sack. I want it delivered to the head of the Roman guards at the barracks— tonight."

"But it is the Sabbath," Nathan reminded him. "I'll break the laws of rest."

"You should care?" Asher gave a disgusted laugh. "Your father could disown you for the trouble you're already in."

Nathan hung his head. "All right," he gulped finally, "I'll go."

"And I will entertain Benjamin for one hour—no more," Asher responded. "Be back by then, or your life is in your own hands."

Nathan stood.

"And don't get caught!" Asher warned. "If you do, I will deny we ever had this conversation."

"How should I do this?" Nathan asked miserably.

"Go to the Antonia by the west gate. Ask for the tribune named Calvin Lentulus. And see only him." Asher picked up his wine and headed for the hallway. "He knows the reason for your coming and won't ask you any questions."

4

STOPPED BY ROMAN GUARDS

The pavement leading to the great Antonia glistened in the fractured light cast down upon it by raised lamps along the curbs. Nathan caught his breath and tightened his belt. Then he started up the steps, his sandals smacking against the stone. Because of his trembling knees he could not stop the sound. Two soldiers centered themselves at the top of the stairs. They were silhouetted in the blazing light of the archway behind them like gnarled olive trees against a sunset sky. The butts of their shoulder-high lances tapped the ground.

"You there. State your business!" one of the men cried out.

Nathan stopped. "To see the tribune named Calvin Lentulus." His voice, answering in Greek, was tremulous on the night air.

The guards exchanged rumbling words. "Approach," they growled.

The guards' eyes and lance tips flashed as they turned inward to clear the way. Nathan went between them with his head down, his chest tight with anxiety. Another soldier, in the field dress of a simple legionary, came in front of him.

"The boy wants a word with the Tribune Calvin Lentulus," a guard called out. "Take him to the officers' quarters."

Nathan followed the soldier through the dark interior of the Antonia's plaza, which seemed as wide as the women's court on the Temple Mount. The bulging muscles of the young Roman's arms and legs momentarily distracted Nathan from his fear. Then they stopped before the door, and the legionary knocked.

"Enter." Nathan heard the faint response inside.

The soldier opened the door and stepped aside. Nathan found himself face-to-face with the officer seated at a table spread with his evening meal. The room was amber-bright from many lamps and the fire that glowed in the brazier. Despite his hatred for Romans, Nathan felt himself caught up in the wonder of his private meeting with a man of such importance.

"A young Jew coming in on the cloaks of night? What shall I do for you?" the tribune asked. His solid, clean-shaven face showed amusement.

Nathan loosened the bag from his belt as he eyed the heathen's food—roast pork, bread, cheese. "I have a delivery. From Asher, a temple chief priest," he said quickly.

"I know very well who Asher is." The officer's face turned hard as sunbaked brick.

Nathan dropped the bag on the table and stepped back.

The tribune put his hand to the sack and pushed it to the edge. "Keep it," he said. "Take it back. Today, I decided—there will be no more bribes."

"Bribes!" Nathan startled himself with the word.

"The mention of bribes surprises you?" the tribune mused. He walked around to Nathan's side of the table and pushed his supper back to clear a seat for himself. "Tell me," he said as he sat on the table's edge, "how is it that you were chosen to carry this most recent of Asher's *gifts?*"

"I . . . I was told you wouldn't ask me questions," Nathan stammered. "I was told you'd understand the reason for my being here."

"So easy, eh?" The tribune raised one eyebrow. He reached for the money sack and pulled its string. The coins jingled as he dug inside. "Ahh, so much silver! Enough to cheer a legion of downhearted, homesick men."

He looked up at Nathan as he tied the bag shut. "But you see, Jew-Boy, I like my job. I like it very much. And I don't wish to be recalled by the governor just for taking coins—and commands—from Judean Jews."

He tossed the bag at Nathan. Nathan nearly collapsed when the weight hit his chest. "I know nothing about any of this," he gasped. "But the money must stay. I cannot take it back."

"You can—and you will!" Calvin Lentulus ordered. "Along with this message. Tell your temple friends that I wash my hands of their cover-up. Remind them of their promise that none of this was to come to the governor's ears. But, in truth, talk about the corpse of Jesus is everywhere. Right here in Jerusalem, I have centurions—tough, professional soldiers—who won't stop saying the man has returned from the dead. No bribe will anchor their tongues. They would turn me in to Rome for taking Asher's money before they would give up saying that Jesus is alive."

Nathan trembled.

"You've understood my message, Jew-Boy?" the Roman asked, firmly planting his fist on Nathan's shoulder. "Then go!"

As if by the magic of the man's gods, the door opened behind Nathan, and he stumbled out into fresh air. The soldier who had led him there now walked behind him with a hand in the small of Nathan's back. Halfway across the courtyard, the soldier jabbed Nathan's ribs. It was not a hand that Nathan felt now, but the cold point of a Roman's short sword.

"I hear everything at the tribune's door," the soldier boasted. "Calvin Lentulus may be against taking bribes, but we legionaries are not."

"What?" Nathan exclaimed. His head jerked back as the soldier grabbed his hair.

"Quiet now. Do as I say, and you'll walk out with your skin."

The legionary pushed him to a dark recess in the

courtyard. Two off-duty guards were playing a dice game close to the warming fire. The men looked up as they approached.

"Romney, Horace—" the legionary whispered. "Be quick, over here. The stakes are a good deal higher in my game."

Without further instruction the three soldiers sprang into action. The first soldier pinned Nathan's hands behind him; the second pushed his lance against Nathan's cheek; the third grabbed the bag at Nathan's belt.

"Filthy, rich Jews!" the guard with the tall spear seethed. "Thinking you can override Rome with your silver. Despite our endless kindness to your people, you never get enough of your own way."

Rome's kindness to Jews? Nathan's temper boiled. He lunged, desperate to free himself of these disgusting hands. But instead of working loose, his desperate thrust jammed the metal spear into his facebone. Nathan toppled toward the pavement. The guard in front tripped him easily, and he hit the ground hard. His cry was like that of a child in pain.

"Oh, without money, see, he has the strength of a locust," the soldiers teased. "Come, come, Little Jew. Don't cry until you've run home."

A voice with authority stopped them. "You, soldiers, resume your rightful activities, or I'll confine all of you to cells."

The three men grunted and moved away without another look in Nathan's direction. He found himself at

the feet of a stern, middle-aged centurion. The Roman offered Nathan a hand, his short metallic tunic rippling as he reached down.

Nathan pressed his palms to the pavement. *All Romans are scum,* he said under his breath. He pushed himself to his feet.

"At least a word of appreciation?" the man suggested as he removed his fluted helmet. "After all, I may have saved your life just now."

Nathan dusted himself off. "Thanks."

"Are you hurt?" the centurion asked.

Nathan thought about the money sack now in the soldiers' hands. "I'm fine," he said. "It was wrong for me to wander in here. I will go."

He started toward the brightly lighted archway where the stern-faced men were still on guard, but suddenly he stopped. A man was crossing the courtyard, going toward the the stairs. It was Stephen, the Greek-speaking Jew.

"Hold up for a moment," the centurion called from behind. Nathan turned, expecting that the command was for him. But the Roman was hurrying to Stephen. "I'd like a word with you, Stephen," the centurion said. "What did you find out tonight when you visited Dorian in prison?"

Dorian! Nathan gasped. Since his troubles with Asher, he had not thought once about the heathen. Now that his own jaw ached from a Roman spear, however, he felt new terror for the boy. At the same time, he wanted nothing more to do with him. His first and only concern was to save himself.

Slowly he walked past the two men, with his face turned downward. He dreaded any words that might come from the Jew or the soldier. If only he could reach the safer darkness of the streets.

A hand tapped his shoulder. It was the centurion's. "Wait," he said. "Let me introduce you to Stephen. He's a friend of mine—and a Jew."

Nathan could not risk this encounter. He had to think quickly, or he'd be forced to identify himself. Glaring at the centurion, he snapped, "If he's a friend of *Roman guards*, he doesn't deserve to be counted as a Jew."

The centurion shook his head. "Now, I know you must meet him, for your own good. He's not like you other Jews. His God knows compassion, not just rules. Stephen—" he said, "perhaps you'd be willing to walk this boy home. He's already had proof that it's not safe to be alone in Jerusalem at night."

Stephen came toward him. Nathan avoided looking into his face. "I can take care of myself, thank you," Nathan said, his eyes directed to the ground. He walked away from the Jew and the centurion to enter the archway. His face suddenly throbbed in the smoky torchlit air. Touching his hand to his cheek, Nathan's fingers felt moist. He looked at them. They were sticky with blood.

"Son, let's have a look at that wound." Nathan turned to find Stephen at his heel. He directed Nathan's face toward the light. "A long slice, but fairly shallow," the Jew concluded. "Praise be to God who watched over you."

Nathan fought within himself to stay hostile toward the man, but Stephen's brown eyes were kind and he was speaking Hebrew now.

"I will go with you into Jerusalem," Stephen insisted. "But first, let me say a few things to the centurion about my meeting with a boy in prison here."

It was his chance to leave, but Nathan lingered. He had to hear their discussion.

"Do you have any say concerning those who guard Dorian's cell?" Stephen asked the centurion.

The centurion shook his head. "I'm afraid not. Those men are not under my command. Why? Has someone been hard on him?"

"Yes," Stephen answered. "He is surrounded by tormentors. The guard assigned there by day continually pulls his sword and tells the boy that thieves leave the Antonia *with both hands gone.*"

Nathan shuddered. *Oh, Dorian, how could you live without hands to carve your works of art?*

"That's an idle threat," the centurion assured Stephen. "I hope you tried to make the boy understand that."

"I did," Stephen replied. "But his real fate, if he is convicted of stealing, may be just as hard. I've spoken to the tribune. He says the boy could be sold into slavery—"

Don't let this be! Nathan's throat pulsed with every word—but he did not let even one sound out.

"Have you tried the Temple?" the centurion suggested. "You're Jewish. Won't the leaders listen to you? Convince them to drop the charges of stealing and take him back to the Sanhedrin for trial."

"He'd do no better there, I'm afraid. Especially if I am the one who speaks for him. As a follower of The Way, I am not well received." He teasingly pointed a finger at the other man. "In part, of course, it has to do with the way I choose my friends."

The centurion laughed. "I think you choose fine friends. The Lord be praised for a man like you, Stephen." He placed a thumb against the belt that held his sword.

Nathan was astonished. A Roman had spoken the name of the One True God!

"If only poor Dorian had chosen his friends as well," the centurion continued.

"I admire the boy," Stephen said. "There's hardly a grown man who would keep silence in such terrible times. Yet Dorian will not name the Jew who loaned him the clothes or the person who went through the Soreg with him. All he will tell me is that it was a young Jew of Jews, one who might suffer greatly if the full truth came to light."

Nathan gasped. *Dorian was keeping himself in danger—just to protect him?*

"And he's willing to face undeserved punishment for this?" the centurion asked with admiration.

"I think so." Stephen nodded. "It tears his heart to think of being a slave. But he says the boy who took him through the forbidden gate gave him his first chance to look for the Eternal God."

"May the Lord show mercy on him for his courage," the centurion said with a shake of his head. "So you've told him everything we have seen and heard about Jesus the Christ?"

"Yes." Stephen rocked on his toes with excitement. "He received the news with a thankful heart. He's ready to live or die in the knowledge that we have been made brothers to the Lord through the suffering of God himself."

Nathan threw his hands to his ears. *Why had he stayed to listen to this? Jesus—the Christ? Men calling themselves brothers to God? Blasphemy! Blasphemy! All of it!*

His anger flared as he turned toward the archway. *Dear Lord of my father, forgive me—for this night!*

He sprang to the stairs and started down two steps at a time. *Forgive me—for taking the carved doves . . .*

He was in the lighted walkway below the gate. *. . . and for bringing the feet of an unclean one onto holy ground. . . .*

He was sobbing in the maze of black streets. *I vow never to break another law!*

Suddenly he was near his own garden gate. Raising his eyes to the roof, he saw that neither Asher nor his father was there. Tomorrow he would have to confront them. He went up to his room, using the outer stairway. Tiptoeing past the servant Shem, who snored on the mat by the inner door, he pulled his garments off and threw himself onto his raised bed.

"Give me some rest," he pleaded. And soon he was asleep.

5

SPOTTED IN THE CROWDS

In his restless sleep Nathan saw again the glowing eyes of a Roman soldier, and even as he awoke from his nightmare a hooked nose and a twisted mouth hung over him.

"Shem!" Nathan shouted when he recognized the ugly face of his own servant. "If you wake me in this way again, I'll have you punished!"

Shem backed to the wall, his knotty fingers nervously folding and unfolding beneath his chin. "Forgive me, young master," he stuttered, "but you were thrashing about so in your sleep. Then I saw your cheek large and red as a pomegranate—"

"A mirror!" Nathan ordered. "Bring me a mirror!" He touched his face as Shem scurried away. It burned and throbbed as he outlined the wound with his finger.

Shem handed the mirror to Nathan and stood wringing his hands.

Nathan sighed at his reflection. "Find me salve and some sort of cosmetic. . . . Go through what remains of my mother's things. There must be something in this house that will cover this."

Without hesitation, Shem disappeared again. Nathan got up from his bed. He dipped his hands into the water basin to cool his arms and face. Suddenly his father's voice sounded on the outside stairway. Nathan jumped into bed, just as his father opened the door.

"Rise up, you sleepyhead. I am ready for the celebration to begin!"

Nathan hid his cheek with the bedcover. He managed a false smile. "As the proverb goes, Father, a loud blessing too early in the morning may be taken as a curse. Please, give me a little time, and I'll greet you in better style."

"Ah, very well," his father said disappointedly. "But be quick! Any moment now, the priests will open the temple gates." Nathan saw that the dark blue sky beyond his father already glowed with dawn.

As his father turned to go, Shem entered the room carrying a tray full of powders. "What's this?" his father questioned, eyeing Nathan again.

The contents on Shem's tray started rattling. Nathan's father brushed past the trembling servant and sat down on Nathan's bed. "Your face," he said with concern. "What has happened to you?"

Nathan saw Shem squeeze his eyes shut in fear of what might come next. Immediately Nathan thought of somehow fixing blame on his bumbling, idiotic servant. But the vow he had formed in the streets last night came rushing back to him. He had promised never to break God's holy law again.

"Father, I will not lie." Nathan began his struggle to speak the truth. He saw Shem's eyes were fastened on him. "This wound was made by the spear of a Roman guard."

"Impossible!" his father raged. "You have not left the house since yesterday."

"But I have. I have been to the Antonia. Asher made me go. It has something to do with the burial of that man called Jesus."

The color drained from his father's cheeks as he touched Nathan's forehead. "It's a fever. You must stay in bed," his father said.

Fear and frustration tightened Nathan's throat. "You must believe me, Father. Asher tried to give money to the tribune as part of some scheme concerning the tomb of Jesus."

"Servant, come here!" Nathan's father ordered.

Shem, even paler than his master, came to the bedside.

"Tell me that my son was here in this room last night. Tell me he was studying the Scriptures he will speak about today, just as Asher said he was."

Shem bowed low, almost touching Benjamin bar Azmon's feet. "Your son is very good. Very good, Master," he responded. "I can say nothing against your son."

"Don't make Shem tell you half-truths," Nathan pleaded. "There is no need for a witness. Last night I went to deliver Asher's money, and it was stolen from me by soldiers. This wound is proof enough of what I say."

"Why did you do this thing?" his father asked angrily.

Nathan's lips moved silently. It had been easier to talk against Asher than to talk against himself. "Because I owed Asher a favor, Father," Nathan struggled. "My uncle has been covering the truth for me. You see, I am the boy who—"

The sound of the temple trumpets burst through the morning air. "Listen!" his father interrupted. "It's time to join the procession in the streets."

"I was the boy who helped a hea—" Nathan said again, almost in a daze.

"Later!" his father insisted. He grabbed Nathan's arms. "I don't want to hear the rest of this. I don't want anything to change this day. You and I are going to the Temple. We are having the feast. What I don't know cannot change these facts. Now dress quickly. And cover that scrape. You are coming with me." Immediately his father left the room.

"Oh, the Holy One favors you," Shem hummed elatedly as he spread out Nathan's clothes. "For a moment, I thought the whole day would be ruined."

"Quiet!" Nathan ordered. Shem pulled the garments over him. Nathan dabbed his own face with salve and then ran down the outside stairs.

His father thrust the two loaves of feast bread into his hands, and they headed out the garden gate. Even in the cool dawn air, the streets were warm with the shoulder-to-shoulder crowds that pressed slowly toward the Temple. Nathan's head swam for lack of air as hundreds of worshipers packed in around him. Here and there women and men practiced snatches of the psalms they would sing within the temple courts.

The sky had brightened from purple to blue before Nathan caught sight of the first temple gate. The crowds moved faster now, and he shuffled along with them. The sound of flute and harp and cymbals drifted over the temple wall as the morning sun lifted a breeze above the excited throng. The first words of the sacred Hallel reached his ears. Nathan joined the hundreds around him who started echoing back responses to the Levite choirs who stood singing inside, near Nicanor's Gate.

"I love the Lord, for he heard my voice." The sound of the Levites came to him.

"He heard my cry for mercy," Nathan sang back with his fellow Jews.

Though his voice seemed lost in the multitude of chants, his father turned to him and smiled. It was a smile of belonging; it thrilled Nathan as they stepped into the women's court. Ahead the fantastic gold-covered walls of the holy sanctuary dazzled his eyes in the clear morning light. The majesty of the singing swelled around him. It seemed to carry him across the courtyard. Before he knew it, his feet were on the stairs of Nicanor's Gate. The women and children were dropping back, but he was going in with Father and the rest of the congregation of Israel. Just before he passed through the columns, a warm hand grabbed his wrist.

"Bena!" he shouted, as he looked over his shoulder. She gave him a quick squeeze. "The Lord bless you," she said with teary eyes. "How everyone in your house has waited for this day when you stand before the altar of the Lord as a man." He nodded gratefully and entered the hazy Court of Israel, which was filled with the smells of incense and burning sacrifices.

"The stone the builders rejected . . . ," the priests around him sang.

". . . has become the most important cornerstone," came back the deep, lusty voices of men responding with zeal.

"The Lord has done this," the Levites shouted.

"It is marvelous in our sight," the now all-male congregation chanted back. Nathan and his father started the twisting dance of the men who went around and around the Court of Israel. Like dust in a whirlwind they were pulled closer and closer to the eye of the celebration—the altar—as their voices rang:

"This is the day the Lord has made. . . .
Let us rejoice and be glad in it."

Nathan danced in the footsteps of his father. He marveled at the wild gestures of joy being made by these usually sober men. He and his father paused, breathless, for a few moments to hand their offerings of bread to a priest. Afterward his father grabbed him, and they continued wheeling around the altar with the crowd.

Then right inside the gate, a few men suddenly

stopped their dance of worship. Nathan and his father slammed against them.

"Stop the ceremony!" these men shouted. "Stop we say! Something extraordinary is going on outside the Temple." Levite guards appeared inside Nicanor's Gate. "No! Keep going," they shouted back to the musicians, who were letting the music die. "Keep everything as planned," they called to the priests who were accepting the bread and grain and lambs the worshipers waved as offerings before the altar.

Nathan's father's face tightened with worry. When the guards spied him, one of them rushed in. "Amarkal," he said breathlessly. "I think you should go outside. Something close to a riot is taking place beyond the temple gates. It's the followers of Jesus. They're preaching about their Christ—all over the streets."

Nathan's father took his hand. He pulled him through the crowds so quickly that Nathan felt he might be torn to shreds before they made their way through the last gate. Outside the Temple people were squeezing together like fish packed into baskets. The guard had been right: everywhere Nathan looked, men were shouting out prophecies from the Scriptures and proclaiming the name of Jesus Christ. Some had even taken to the rooftops to do their preaching.

"Listen," Nathan gasped to his father. "Different ones are speaking in Greek and Latin and Hebrew, and yet they are all saying exactly the same thing."

His father's eyes were wide with worry. "I see Asher over there," he said. "Let's get to him."

When he saw them coming, Asher shouted, "This is some sort of trick!" He wiped beads of perspiration from his forehead. "But we'll get to the bottom of it. There's the leader of the bunch—over by that wall."

Again Nathan felt his feet and arms being twisted in opposite directions as the three formed a caravan through the masses. Chants of "Drunkards! Drunkards!" rose from scoffers in the crowds.

The stocky, full-bearded Jew with sun-scorched arms, who had attracted Asher's attention, was waving his hands to stop the tauntings. He had no success on the ground. Tucking the hem of his tunic between his legs and into his belt, as a common laborer would do before starting his work, he scaled the wall that separated one of the better homes from the dust of the street.

Now that he towered over the crowd, he started yelling. "Listen carefully. Let me explain. These men are not drunk as you claim. No—what is happening in your presence was predicted long ago by our prophet Joel. 'In the last days, God says, I will pour out my Spirit on all people. Your sons and your daughters will speak prophecies, and your old men will dream dreams. Even on my servants, the Spirit will come. There will be wonders from the heaven and signs on the earth below. . . . And everyone who calls on the name of the Lord will be saved!' "

"Who is that man?" Nathan's father said to Asher. "He looks like a hired hand, but he speaks like a scribe."

Asher shook his head. "That's Simon Peter from Galilee. He and his brother were followers of Jesus. How

I wish they had gone back to their fishing boats after their leader died."

Nathan could not keep himself from studying the rage on Asher's face. His uncle caught his gaze.

"What makes you look at me like that?" Asher snapped. "I'm a priest. Isn't it my responsibility to protect the faithful ones from such human wolves?"

"But this man is speaking about King David and our prophets," Nathan said. "How do you know he is not a good Jew?"

Asher looked at him indignantly. "Good Jews, nephew, are inside the Temple. They are there singing in front of the altar of the Lord."

Turning to Benjamin, Asher crossed his arms. "Well, Benjamin, any suggestions as to what should be done?"

Nathan's father shrugged. "It's hard to believe that men would preach this powerfully on behalf of a dead man."

"Come, come," Asher chided. "They know the people will be here for the Feast of Harvest. They have an eager audience."

Nathan's father sighed. "Before Jesus died, Jerusalem buzzed with other false teachers and rumors. They are all forgotten in time. Perhaps we should direct our attention back to temple affairs, and let these men preach to the heathen if they want to."

"But these men come in the name of our God and use our prophets!" Asher roared. "This false teaching about a Messiah stirs up all the people. It makes otherwise civil Jews discontent."

Even above Asher's ranting, Nathan could hear Simon Peter speaking: "Let all Israel know this," the man was shouting. "God has made this Jesus, whom you crucified, both Lord and Christ!"

A man beside Nathan suddenly tore his robe. Another fell on his face and threw dust upon his head. A wailing started like that heard in the streets during funerals.

"See! See what I mean!" Asher growled. "People are losing their senses."

Simon Peter raised his voice louder still.

"Repent! Be baptized in Jesus' name so that your sins will be forgiven. So that you will be filled with God's Spirit. This promise is to you and your children!"

Nathan stood transfixed at the power of the words. This was no ordinary rumor being passed to excite the people against the Romans.

His father turned him away. "We've seen enough of this. Let's go," he said.

As they pushed back toward the Temple, Nathan saw Stephen directly in the street before him. Quickly he put a hand to his injured cheek and moved behind his father. But it was not in time. Stephen had seen him clearly. The man hurried up to talk with him.

"I know you—from last night," Stephen said excitedly, while Nathan's father watched in horror. "What a wonder that you are here! You are witnessing a miracle.

We have been waiting and praying for the Spirit of Jesus to come upon us, and now he is here!"

Nathan's father grabbed Nathan. "I said we have heard enough," he said tightly, half to Nathan and half to Stephen. "And as for this man, Nathan, he cannot possibly know you."

Stephen gave Nathan a worried look. Then he went on to join the listening crowds at the foot of the wall.

"I do know him." Nathan struggled for a way to tell his father the truth. "You see—" Asher's approach cut his words from the air.

"Nathan should stay away from men like that one!" Asher said to Benjamin.

His father sighed. "I agree. Nathan, for your own good and the sake of the Temple, I don't want you associating with these followers of The Way."

"But I wasn't associating with them," Nathan said.

"Good," his father answered. "Then let's go home to see about this feast of yours."

6

SPEAKING THE TRUTH

Fish and fruits, nuts and fig cakes, olives and delicately flavored locusts all filled Nathan's dish at the feast that afternoon. Around him more than fifty guests reclined at the tables enjoying the meal. Their laughter and happy talk swelled to the roof of the mansion's large upper room.

Nathan's father ate beside him. He was keeping him occupied with light conversation, and Nathan knew as both parent and Amarkal, he was trying to prevent him from worrying about the moments that would follow the feast. Then Nathan would have to rise to read the Scriptures and make his short speech on God's ten holy laws in front of this large group. While they were talking, Nathan saw Asher get up from another table. He marched directly to Nathan's side and motioned for him and his father to leave their couches.

Behind the dark draperies that screened the weekday serving tables from the hall, Asher confronted them in a low, worried voice. "There are some priests at this feast, brother, who are spreading ugly rumors about your son. I do not think it is wise for Nathan to stay within view of these men."

"Not stay?" Benjamin exclaimed. "These people are our friends, Asher. This party is for my son. How could you possibly suggest this?"

Asher plucked at his beard. "Even as I was dining with Obed and some of the others," he explained, "they were pointing out how closely Nathan resembles the boy who was seen with the heathen in the Court of Israel."

Nathan's breath caught in his throat. His father groaned as he looked at Nathan. "How can this be?"

Nathan's tongue was rough and dry with silence.

"I did not want a confrontation, son," his father said steadily. Wrinkles skirted his lips and eyes in ways that Nathan had not seen before. "But now, I must have the truth from you. Tell me everything." He raised his chin slightly as if bracing himself for the coming words.

Asher popped his head out through the slit between curtains. He pulled it back. "Benjamin, you can't possibly choose this moment for discussion. Think of our guests. Everyone's wondering . . ."

"I want to know the facts. I want them now," Nathan's father said coolly.

Nathan sighed. "What is being said . . . is true," he struggled. "I am that Jew."

"It can't be true!" Asher exclaimed.

Nathan looked at his uncle with wild surprise. "Why do you say that? You know everything about it! Why are you saying that you do not know?"

Benjamin looked from Nathan to Asher. "What is going on? Asher! I demand the truth!"

"Shhh . . ." Asher put his hand on Benjamin's shoulder. "Remember—the guests. Believe me. It would be better for you *not* to know everything."

"This concerns my son!" Benjamin whispered angrily.

Nathan could not hold back. "I led the heathen through the gate, Father. He *was* the boy you saw in the bird market. Everything inside me wishes that I hadn't, but I did, and what is done is done."

His father grabbed Nathan's arms. With a violent shake he pleaded, "Why? Why did you do this?"

Nathan looked to the ceiling. "I'm not sure," he said. "At first I thought it was the trade he offered—a look into the Temple in exchange for two small beautifully carved doves!"

Asher slapped his cheeks. "God of our Fathers! Now idols have come into this! What next!"

"No!" Nathan protested. "Believe me, Father! They weren't idols to me! I don't even have those things anymore. And it wasn't because of the carvings that I led him in. It was . . . it was because . . ."

His father squeezed his wrist. "Tell me the truth!"

The hurt in his father's face sliced Nathan's heart. "I can hardly speak of it now," he choked. "But somehow I felt shamed when the boy talked to me about my religion. Somehow he made me feel that . . . well, that he really wanted to know the Eternal One, and that we Jews were the ones who were keeping him from finding God."

"And that's why you took him through the Soreg?" Asher finished for him.

"I know it seems senseless now," Nathan stammered. "But somehow it seemed right then." He managed to look at his father.

Tears filled Benjamin's eyes. Nathan bit his lip. It was awful to see his father so upset. He reached for his father's arm. "I am sorry," he whispered. "Forgive me for what I've done."

Asher broke in. "Benjamin, you've got to get back to your table."

Nathan's father crossed his arms. "Just one more thing. Tomorrow, Nathan, you will go before the Sanhedrin. You will tell what you have done, and even if it means flogging—yes, flogging—" He stopped as a sudden gasp of despair escaped with his breath. "You will take the punishment you deserve."

"All this can be avoided, I'm telling you," Asher interrupted, "if you just let Nathan slip away now until this thing blows over. Say that he has suddenly taken ill."

Nathan's father turned on him angrily. "God detests lying—especially from the lips of the amarkal's sons and priests!" He was trembling with rage. "Nathan is not ill. I will not lie even to protect my son!"

Asher grabbed his brother's robe. "Benjamin, I beg you. Do not let your son go through with the ceremony today. After he reads the Scriptures at this feast, he will be formally accepted in the congregation. From that moment on he will have to endure the letter of the law as a

Jewish man. But before that moment he is still considered a child—Don't you see? Keep him from this ceremony. Protect him from being punished by the Sanhedrin."

Benjamin closed his eyes.

Asher gave Nathan a thin, nervous grin. "Brother, we both know the importance of keeping Nathan in good standing at the Temple. After all, someday he will be in line for your position." He brought his palms together. "So, well, I already gave my word to the leaders that Nathan was not even inside the Temple yesterday."

"What a liar you are!" Benjamin glared. "I want you out of my house this instant."

"Brother, think what you're doing," Asher pleaded. "I have been working for Nathan's good. I'll leave, as you wish, but only if Nathan comes with me."

Nathan's father answered Asher with a word. "Never!" Then he took hold of Nathan's shoulder. "Within the hour, son, you will publicly embrace the law. You will join the congregation of Israel."

Painfully his father pulled back the curtain, and Nathan walked out before the faces of the guests who were waiting for him. At his father's direction he moved to the place of honor. Obed, a chief priest and friend of Asher, walked up through the silent audience and presented Nathan the scroll.

With trembling hands Nathan removed the protective cloths from it. He took the stiff, precious parchment which had been exposed and put it to his lips. He kissed God's Holy Word, and with all eyes fixed upon him, he unrolled the book and began to read the portion expected of him:

" 'Hear, O Israel: The LORD our God, the LORD is one. Love the LORD your God with all your heart and with all your soul and with all your strength. . . .' " Then he rolled the scroll forward to read the ten great laws God had given them. His voice stopped as his eyes found the words. The jagged Hebrew letters stabbed out toward him. Laws that God had first written on stone with the finger of his hand now seemed to be carved on the tender flesh of Nathan's own heart. He realized he was standing there taking fast gulps of hot air. He struggled to read. But no sounds moved from his lips.

Within the crowd he saw Obed's frown, Asher's nervous shifting, his father's pained eye. Suddenly he laid the scroll on the table. "I . . . I am not worthy to read the Holy Word," he stammered.

Before he could stop himself he had run out of the banquet room and down into the street. The hot evening air hit Nathan like a knife. It warned him that he was cutting himself off from everything safe and precious to him: his home, his father, his life as a Jew. Several houses away he stopped and looked back. Perhaps his father would leave his guests. Perhaps he would come after him.

Nathan stood at the end of his street until the sun melted into the horizon and the air had cooled. But as gray shadows grouped around him, they sealed his fear. His father was letting him go. He would need to find a place to spend the night.

With a heavy heart Nathan walked downhill into the narrow pathways of the Lower City. The shops and workshops and artisans' homes lay as tight as grain in the heads of ripened wheat. He had never been alone in this part of the city at night. No richer than a beggar now, he eyed the doorways, looking for a place where he might rest. The first notch he found in a wall was occupied by a drunkard; the second still held the stench of drifters who had come before him. And before he could find a third, a pack of wild street dogs was on his heels chasing him deeper into the unfamiliar territory. Finally he lost the pack and stopped to catch his breath. His chest burned as he slid against a potter's shed.

Suddenly his head was being banged against the bricks. "Your fine tunic! The belt you wear!" a stinking, toothless robber growled. "I want them now!"

Nathan grew faint as the man yanked his garments off. When his head cleared, the thief had disappeared, and he was left with only the thin short tunic that he wore next to his skin. Shivering, he bit his knuckles to keep from crying. Even his precious ring was gone! At his feet lay a dark cloak. He picked up the rough, vile-smelling robe and pulled it around his shoulders. *God of my Fathers*, he begged as he fell to his knees, *have mercy on me, or I will be dead by morning.*

7

ALONE ON THE STREETS

Beneath the weight of the beggar's coat, Nathan walked toward the Temple Mount, the one place he could think of that offered comfort. At the southwest corner of the Temple, a huge archway of stairs rose from the streets of the Lower City. Nathan's mind was fixed on going underneath the bridge that was formed by this gigantic walkway. There beneath the stairs and against the temple wall, he might at last find a place to rest.

But when Nathan arrived, his heart sank. Fires already glowed in the shadow of the stairway. The pavement was filled with others who were spending the night there in the streets. From the psalms the people sang, he guessed they were Jewish travelers waiting out the end of the Sabbath before starting their journey home. Sadly Nathan turned away.

A small dark dog came rushing at him. Nathan yelled and kicked out at it. Even as his heel was in the air, he stopped. It was only a puppy, one with sad wet eyes. The young dog nuzzled him, and Nathan patted its soft, flat head. The pup began to wiggle with affection. A little girl from the campfire toddled out to the dog and caught it by the neck. She tried, but could not drag the puppy back with her.

"Here," Nathan offered. "I'll help you. Show me where your mother is." The girl gave him a little smile and grabbed onto the cloak at Nathan's knee. Nathan scooped up the dog. They walked a short way until they met a woman from the group of evening campers.

"Oh, thank you," she said. "I turned my back for one moment, and they were gone."

Nathan nodded. He let the dog down and pried himself loose from the girl's tight little fist. The sight of an orange cooking fire in the street and the aroma of stew weakened him with homesickness.

A lanky man with short curly hair joined them. "Man, come sit with us," he said in a hearty voice to Nathan. "Looks like you might be in need of a resting place."

Nathan shrugged nervously and followed him into the circle of firelight. Around him men were reclining on their elbows and talking with each other. Women were serving supper or rocking sleepy children while singing to them. Overhead, the wide span of the temple stairway protected all the people who planned to spend the night in the street.

The mother of the little girl came back to Nathan. She handed him thick chunks of bread and cheese. Nathan took it with thanks as he sat down, though he wasn't the least bit hungry. Uneasily he looked around.

The woman's husband noticed his hesitation. "It's fine to eat with us." He smiled. "Go on. From the condition of your cloak, I'd judge you haven't had real food for a week."

Nathan looked down at himself in shame. Of course, without cap or robe, he looked like a heathen beggar. "Ahh . . . I'm a Jew," he stammered.

The man's grin widened, though his eyes showed surprise. "Well, so are we." He nodded. "Now, relax and eat."

Nathan frowned. "But a Jew doesn't eat without washing his hands."

The man's mouth dropped open. "You really are a Jew, aren't you?" he said with a puzzled laugh. He looked around and called to a youth who was skirting the light of the fire. "Young man, could you hand me my wife's water jar over there?"

The boy came with the water. The face behind the clay jar caught Nathan's attention. "Dorian!" he cried with disbelief. "Dorian! How can it be you?"

Dorian's dark eyes widened, and the water jar crashed to the pavement. "What! I know you, too," he shouted. "From the Temple. You're—" he stopped sharply.

"Nathan," Nathan supplied breathlessly, moving away from the puddle made by the broken water vessel. Because of the sound of broken pottery, all eyes were on them.

"You two know each other?" the man who was standing near them asked.

"Yes!" Dorian exclaimed. "He is the Jew who first started my search for God."

Nathan looked away. "You're supposed to be in prison. I heard you'd probably be sold as a slave."

"It's a wonderful act of God!" Dorian shouted with his hands in the air. "Today the tribune freed me into the care of a Jewish man, and all afternoon I have been with him as God himself moved through the town. By the Spirit of Jesus, many came to believe. There is a God and he has a purpose for us!"

A shadow of anger darkened Nathan's heart. It must have shown on his face, for Dorian leaned close with a look of surprise. "What is it? Why aren't you ready to share my joy?"

Nathan's throat ached as the anger grew. "I risked everything for you!" He clenched his teeth. "Look at me. In beggar's robes. I traded my house, my father, my life for you. But you are free without my help. I could have kept my mouth shut! But now I've lost everything. For nothing."

Dorian threw his arms around Nathan. "Then you did care about me after all. You didn't take me to the Temple just because of the carvings I gave you. You really felt for me." He raised his arms toward the heavens. "Thanks be to you, God.

"In prison I sealed my lips to protect you, Nathan," he said, continuing to rejoice. "And I learned to pray for you too. Now look what the Holy Spirit of God has done."

Nathan punched Dorian in the ribs so hard that the

boy landed in the dust. "Shut your heathen mouth!"
Nathan roared while Dorian sat shaking his head to clear
his vision. "You shame God with your reckless tongue.
And you have shamed me too. I curse the day I met
you!" He spit at Dorian's feet to punctuate his words.

Dorian slowly rose and brushed his drab tunic.
"Nathan," he panted, "please. You don't understand. I
have met God. This would have never happened if I had
not met you."

Before Nathan could protest, the boy put his hands
to his mouth and shouted. "Stephen. Over here. I have
found the one who set my steps toward Christ."

"I did no such thing!" Nathan protested. "I follow
God. I have nothing to do with false Messiahs." Suddenly the wound on his cheek, which he had not thought
about all afternoon, started throbbing again.

"This is the boy who led me through the Soreg,"
Dorian boasted as Stephen neared. "His name's Nathan."

Stephen smiled. "Nathan," he said with satisfaction. "So we meet for a third time. Surely God himself
must have his reasons for this."

Nathan ignored Stephen's words and turned angrily
on Dorian. "Tell the whole world that we've been in the
Temple together." His voice cracked with emotion. "It
can do no harm now! I am as homeless and as poor as
you are because of the time we spent together." He
walked away from the fire so that no one could see the
tears fall on his cheeks.

Nathan felt Dorian's hand on his waist. "Oh, how I

have hurt you, Nathan. I see it now for the first time. You truly *have* lost everything for me. No wonder my friendship seems worthless to you."

Through his tears of anger, Nathan saw that Dorian's eyes were wet, too.

After a long silence Stephen joined them. "Nathan, why do you come here in a beggar's robe? This morning I saw you with an amarkal. I assumed he was your father."

Nathan's lip quivered. "He is . . . but he will probably never speak to me again. Ever since I met Dorian things have been going wrong. I was to join the congregation of Israel today, but I didn't. Instead, I ran away from everything—to nothing. A thief even stole the clothes off my back. . . ."

With a steady hand Stephen raised Nathan's trembling chin. "Look at me, son," he said. "I think God's Spirit is moving in your heart."

"God's Spirit rests in the great Holy of Holies inside the Temple," Nathan spouted angrily. "How can you say that God moves inside men's hearts?"

"Because God himself has told us this," Stephen replied. "Jesus Christ made this promise to his disciples: 'You know the Spirit of Truth . . . for he lives with you and will be *in* you.' "

"I'm not interested in the words of some poor carpenter," Nathan protested wearily.

Stephen held out open hands. "Then listen to the words of your own prophet Isaiah. 'He was despised and rejected by men, a man of sorrows, familiar with suffering. . . . We were quick to say that God himself was against him. In truth he was pierced for our transgressions. He was crushed because of our sin. The punishment that brought us peace was upon him. And by his wounds we are healed.' "

Nathan sighed. "You think this speaks of your Jesus on the cross, don't you?"

"Yes, yes I do," Stephen told him. "You were at the Temple today for the Pentecost celebration," he observed. "You saw for yourself how the Spirit of God works in the hearts of men and women who heard our message."

Pentecost! Stephen's use of the Greek name for the Jewish festival made Nathan too angry for words. Stephen looked at him and started humming. Then he added the words:

> *Open for me the gates of righteousness;*
> *I will enter and give thanks to the LORD.*
> *This is the gate of the LORD*
> *through which the righteous may enter.*
> *I will give you thanks, for you answered me;*
> *you have become my salvation. . . .*

"You know the Hallel by heart?" Nathan said with surprise.

"Yes, every line of it, and today as never before I celebrate every word!" Stephen exclaimed. "Remember the next phrase, the one about the stone that the builders reject?"

"The one that becomes the most important corner-stone?"

Stephen nodded. "Jesus Christ has become like that for me. Rejected by so many, but precious to everyone who believes in him. Doesn't it amaze you that God would choose this very day to pour out his Spirit among us—while these words from the Hallel are on so many lips. But who was paying enough attention to even think about it? God *is* in our midst, yet most people just go on living their own way."

Nathan dragged his sandal across the stone street. "It's clear that we hold very few ideas in common," he said. "I think I should go."

Stephen smiled sadly. "Go where?" he asked, but he didn't wait for a reply. "Dorian and I were going to camp here in the street with these people. So many have come to know Jesus Christ today. But a little while ago, other followers who live in Jerusalem invited us to stay with them. Why don't you come too? Share our food and shelter. And see for yourself if there is enough evidence to believe that God has sent the Messiah to us."

8

A TEST OF WILLS

The single small lamp still flickered from its niche in the brick wall when Nathan awoke. He squinted and sat up to look around the narrow, sunless room that had been his nighttime shelter for many days. For a moment he was unable to tell if morning had come. Then along one wall he saw the sleeping mats of his companions already rolled up for the day. He was the last one out of bed—again, and he scolded himself for it as he jumped up to store his own mat with the others.

Hurriedly he washed his hands and face in the earthen basin beside the door. As the cool water trickled through his fingers he wondered about time. How many nights had he slept here in the cleared-out stable room of this simple city home? How many times had the followers of The Way, who shared this space with him, left for their daily activities before he even climbed off his mat?

Laughter and bits of conversation let him know that

the house was not as empty this morning as it usually was. Slipping into the plain tunic that had been loaned to him by the owner of the home, he walked up the two steps that divided the stable from the larger, slightly brighter, living-cooking room.

"Morning, Nathan," the woman of the house said. Her dress was simpler than any Bena ever wore, but her eyes were just as kind as those of his servant. She handed him a bowl of olives and a string of figs. "For you and Stephen and Dorian," she said lightly. "My husband and all the other believers have already left for the day."

Nathan winced at her words. He was not a believer, and she knew that. Her glance caught his silent remark. "I'm sorry, Nathan. It's just hard to remember that you're not a follower. We've come to love you so much—yet you can't bring yourself to be one of us. Perhaps, one day you will. . . ."

"Perhaps." Nathan said things like this to ease the guilt he felt in accepting her hospitality but not her ways. The followers were so kind to him. In his weaker moments he wished he, too, believed that Jesus the Carpenter had been raised from the dead. If someone, somehow, could show him that the resurrection were true, then he *would* be a follower of Jesus, one of those who called him the Messiah.

Carrying breakfast into his friends, he sat down with them on the floor. Stephen smiled and whispered a blessing over the food, one that Nathan had heard since boyhood. As soon as Stephen finished, Dorian's hand was in the bowl, but he stopped before his fingers touched the food.

"I'm sorry, Nathan," he said, drawing his hand to his side. "I forgot you must eat first—because a Jew doesn't share the bowl with Gentiles. I just forgot—"

Nathan glared at him while he took his portion.

Dorian's eyes still danced happily. "I didn't mean that in a bad way," he explained. "I'm just speaking the facts. You know how I feel about you. You're like a brother—even with your rules."

Dorian took some olives and passed the bowl to Stephen, but the man shook his head. "What's bothering you, brother Stephen? I can tell when something's on your mind."

Stephen chuckled. "This is very true, Dorian, very true." He drew his lips together. "Many of the believers are fasting and praying for Peter and John. Yesterday the temple leaders arrested them again and put them back in prison."

Nathan's hands tingled. His father and uncle were a part of this. They were the ones arresting those who had, in the course of his stay here, become his close friends.

Stephen put his hands together. "When the Sanhedrin meets today I think these two disciples will be tried. Since I plan to teach about Jesus in the Court of the Gentiles, it might be possible for me to get some news on them. Until then, I know it is important for us to fast and pray."

Immediately Dorian dropped his two remaining

olives into the bowl. "Then I will fast and pray too," he said with conviction. "And I will go with you to the Temple." He looked at Nathan. "Why don't you come, too?"

Nathan sighed. He had not set foot on the Temple Mount since moving in with the believers. It was too risky to have to face his father or Asher or any of their friends.

Stephen stood. "I understand, Nathan," he said. "Besides, as usual, there's much work for you here. The vats of grain we have collected for the Greek-speaking widows need to be divided into weekly rations. Several sisters in the faith should be here soon to start this work. But I need you to manage the scales and make some records since no one else will be here who can write or work with figures."

Nathan nodded with half a smile. This had become the pattern of his life. While Stephen, the original disciples of Jesus, and the many newly converted believers spent their days on the streets proclaiming their good news of the Christ, Nathan worked in this house measuring out supplies and doing the work of a scribe for those followers of The Way who could neither read nor write.

Dorian joined Stephen at the steps going down into the stable room, which separated the family's living quarters from the street. "We'll try to be back early enough to repair a roof or two in the Lower City, in addition to delivering some of that grain," Stephen promised.

"It tires us just to hear your plans for one day," Dorian teased, pushing his fingers to his temples.

Stephen bopped the boy lightly on his head as the two disappeared into the street.

It was lonely being left with the women, Nathan soon decided as he worked in the small outdoor terrace. He worked an hour or more carrying and weighing out the huge pottery containers filled with grain. Four women, young and old, sat around him filling up baskets and jars with the rations he divided. They were good at talking among themselves, but he had few words to say. Suddenly he heard Dorian's excited voice.

"You've got to come," the boy gasped. "A miracle has freed Peter and John! When the guards came for them, they were already back in the temple courts giving praise to God!"

Wonder and curiosity overrode Nathan's fear. Instantly he was in the streets with Dorian. Both boys raced up the temple stairway amid the shouts from the crowds. In the middle of the Court of the Gentiles, Dorian elbowed his way to the front so he could see what was happening. But Nathan hung back. Already he saw the danger he might be in.

Several Levites and priests, including Asher, were combing the crowds to find the Jews who had been the first disciples of Jesus. Nathan hid his face from a Levite who passed him by to pull Andrew and Thomas from the shouting, crying throngs. Peter and John were already in chains again at the center of the courtyard. And when eight or nine other men had been rounded up, the temple guards herded them all away.

"They're taking them to trial!" a woman beside

Nathan wailed. A friend caught her by the shoulders. "Shhhh now," she comforted. "We must be strong and pray that their courage will not fail."

Nathan only halfheartedly listened to her words. Other thoughts were piercing his mind. He pressed through the crowd, walking toward Asher, though his knees weakened with each step. At once his uncle spied him. Nathan saw his eyes narrow.

"So you show yourself again," Asher huffed. "What brings you here?"

"I volunteer to speak for those men," Nathan said, pointing to the disciples who were being led to the council room. He had steadied his voice, but his words still cracked before he finished them.

Asher looked around. There were witnesses—Jewish leaders and believers in Jesus—who had heard Nathan's words. Nathan knew the embarrassment he was bringing to his uncle.

"Leave!" Asher warned.

"I make no claim to be a follower, Uncle. But I know these men. I have stayed with some of them. I tell you, they do not deserve to be treated this way."

Asher stepped up to Nathan and pressed a finger into his chest. "I know your father warned you not to associate with these followers. Why do you add shame upon shame by continuing to disobey him?"

"They took me in and protected me when I had no home," Nathan told him. "And I saw more compassion among these believers in a week than I witnessed among temple leaders in my whole lifetime."

"You *have* a home if you would come to it!" Asher retorted. "Even now, your father mourns your leaving like a death."

Nathan squeezed his eyes shut. He had not planned on hearing such words of pain. Even so, he would not stop now. "I won't think of coming home until one thing is settled for me," he said.

"What's that?" his uncle snapped.

"I must know what makes the tomb of Jesus empty." Nathan steadied his breathing. "Was his body stolen, as the temple officials tell us? Or did the Lord of Heaven raise him from the dead? When I have the answer to that I will know whether to seek my father's forgiveness for what I have done—or stay with these believers."

Nathan heard the surprised, fluttering whispers of the crowd around them.

Asher's face was red as wine. "You know the answer to that! I told you myself. Those men stole Jesus' body. You have my word on it."

"Your word?" Nathan let out an angry laugh. "The same word you gave to the leaders when you told them I was not in the Temple on the day the Gentile boy came through the gates?"

From the corner of his eye Nathan saw that Dorian had joined him. He turned and raised Dorian's hand with his, as the people watched with astonishment. "This is my friend, Asher. The boy who came through the Soreg with me!"

Asher clenched his teeth, but Nathan kept speaking. "Now I will go to the Sanhedrin, Uncle, and I'll tell them *everything* I know."

Asher lunged at Nathan, grabbed his free arm, and whisked him away from Dorian to the temple treasury. His fingernails sank into Nathan's skin. "I can stop your plan," he warned, "and I will. You see, there is no way you can serve as a witness in the disciples' trial. You forget, Nathan, the Temple still looks upon you as a child. The leaders will not let you present evidence for someone else."

Nathan dropped his head. *Why had he not remembered this?*

"Even so," Asher went on with an awful smile, "I will let you see what is left of the trial. I think I know how it will end, and I want you to be there watching. What you see will clear your thinking. Even when you are a man, you will never consider testifying against me again."

Asher forced Nathan to stand outside the door of the courtroom and listen. Nathan knew the voice of the speaker. It was the high priest Caiaphas, leader of the Sanhedrin. "You men were warned not to teach in the name of Jesus," he was shouting, "but still you fill Jerusalem with your talk!"

"We must obey God rather than men." The strong voice of Peter interrupted. "The God of our fathers raised Jesus from the dead—whom you had killed by hanging him on a tree. God exalted him to his own right hand as Prince and Savior—so that Israel could find repentance and forgiveness. We are witnesses to these things. And so is the Spirit of God who dwells in those who obey him."

Nathan heard benches creak and voices rise as Peter's testimony whipped the Sanhedrin into an uproar. Just then Asher pushed Nathan through the open door. "Quick, to the back corner of the room," he whispered. "I want you to witness this, but I don't want you to be seen. Hurry, before Caiaphas quiets this crowd."

Asher squeezed Nathan to the wall and stood in front of him. Finally the waves of shouting ebbed. He could see enough across his uncle's shoulder to know that the white-haired Gamaliel was rising in the group. He stood in the semicircle of leaders who had again taken their seats in the wide, white room.

"Men of Israel, consider carefully what you intend to do with these preachers." The elder spoke in the steady, strong voice that was loved by Jews everywhere. "Other leaders—men such as Theudas and Judas the Galilean—came posing as Messiah, and think what history teaches us of them. When they died, their followers scattered into nothingness. In light of this, consider your present case. I advise you, let the followers of Jesus go. Unless their activity is spurred by God himself, they will fail. But if their activity *is* of God, then know that you will not be able to stop them. In fact, you will actually find yourself fighting *against* the Eternal One."

The room rumbled with mixed responses to Gamaliel's advice. After many had spoken, Caiaphas called out the decision: "Each man will be whipped! Each will be warned not to speak the name of Jesus anymore!"

Again the seats of the courtroom groaned and scraped as the council adjourned. Many of the seventy officials went out to a small walled plaza near the council room, between the Gentile courtyard and the public streets. Asher kept an iron grip on Nathan's wrist and forced him to the same area. "Now stand and watch this," he challenged angrily. "Let this be your warning never to be caught disobeying temple rule."

Twelve strong hazans, one for each follower, stripped the disciples to their waists. They hooked the bound hands of each man high onto a whipping post. Each disciple stretched silently, his back bare, his feet apart on the pavement, his head bowed unnaturally between his elbows and the wooden pole. Nathan saw them straining to look at one another with quiet eyes.

On command the hazans stepped up to the short raised platforms behind the men. Each took hold of a four-stranded whip. The captain saw they were ready. "Begin!" he shouted.

"One!" The first lash cracked. "Two!" Another short, hard, practiced drive went against flesh. "Three—"

With each awful smack someone in the crowd called out, "Speak no more of Jesus! Speak no more of Jesus!" until the disciples' bodies sagged and were covered with red and bloody stripes.

Nathan turned way, with vomit rising from his stomach. "Why is this being done? Don't make them suffer. . . ."

But Asher grabbed his neck and straightened him. "They are troublemakers," he said. "You watch every lash. Then you will not find yourself in their position."

Nathan squinted in distress. The men were forced to turn so that the whips would catch their arms and chests as well as their backs. Young John's head rolled in agony as the leather straps tore at one shoulder and then the other. Nathan shut his eyes. *Thirty-nine lashings were laid on each disciple. Over one hundred fifty purple, weeping welts raised up across each body.*

Nathan held his head when the horror ended. A temple officer with a knife walked out and cut the disciples loose one by one. Andrew. James. Peter. John. The rest of them. Each fell free with a gasp of pained relief. They staggered toward one another, wilted and bleeding, but conscious and able to stand.

"The Lord be praised! The Lord be praised!" These words started echoing among them. "We have been strong for him! The Lord be praised!"

A frown knit Asher's eyebrows. "You've been here long enough, Nathan," he said. "Now I will take you home."

But Nathan pulled away. He walked to the disciples. Gently he put John's bleeding arm across his own neck. "I'm going to help my friends, Asher. I watched them suffer as you wanted me to. And you were right—they showed me everything I need to know." He looked at the Jewish crowd. He saw his father watching him, but he turned away. "Come on, brother," he said to John. "I will help you to the street." He led him to the gate. As soon as they were outside, many followers ran up to help.

The heat of the afternoon sun flamed the men's swollen flesh as the procession of believers limped along. John drew in sharp, hard breaths as Nathan supported him on the way.

At the direction of some of the women, the injured men were taken into the believers' homes. Nathan's shoulders ached with fatigue when he finally lowered John onto his own mat in the house where he stayed. John's brother James and a disciple named Philip were also there. And Stephen was kneeling beside Thomas, pouring a mixture of oil and wine into that disciple's hot, red wounds. One of the women who had joined them carried a bowl of medicine to Nathan. He dipped a cloth into it. With a shaking hand he trickled the liquid onto John's shoulder. The man groaned, and Nathan pulled back. But John encouraged him, "Go on. It's not so bad as I made it sound. I'm grateful for your help."

Nathan wet his cloth once more, touched it to skin, and waited for the young man's wincing to subside. Each time the bowl passed by, Nathan took his turn at washing the wounds. When he moved to the angry stripes lacing the disciple's chest, John questioned him between gasping sighs. "I don't even know your name, friend. Have you just recently become a follower?"

Nathan bit his lip. "I . . . I'm not a follower," he confessed. "But you see, I admire you all greatly. And it's only that, well, I don't know what to believe about the empty tomb. I've been told that you followers stole the body, and I half believed it until I saw you being flogged today. Now I think you would not have endured all this for some dead corpse." Nathan stopped. "Forgive me," he breathed. "I'm troubling you in your time of need."

John took the stained rag into his own hands. His eyes closed, and his face formed a smile. "It's no trouble to answer about the tomb of Christ. I was there myself. It *was* empty. With my own eyes I have seen the living Lord. . . ."

Nathan's heart throbbed in his throat. "It's true, then," he said. "It's true!"

John's head drifted back until it touched the wall. "Thanks be to God. It's true." The exhausted disciple sank into an exhausted sleep.

"Then I believe you, Jesus!" Nathan whispered.

Pulling the cloth from John's fingers, Nathan draped it over the bowl. He went to Stephen, who was sitting on the floor near Thomas. Stephen's eyes were shut, and his blood-splotched hands were clasped against his chest. Nathan sat down at his feet, hardly able to wait.

Presently Stephen flexed his fingers and looked at Nathan. "I didn't know you were sitting here, my young friend." He leaned forward and squeezed Nathan's arm. "Are you all right? I saw you with John. He has some deep wounds."

Nathan nodded. "He's sleeping now. Stephen, I want to tell you—I've committed myself to Jesus!"

Stephen drew Nathan to his chest. "Thanks be to

God!" He squeezed him tightly. "Now live for God, Nathan bar Benjamin," he said with the emotion of a father. "Live for God."

Nathan glanced around the room. "Where's Dorian?"

"He's gone back to his grandfather," Stephen replied. "I was just praying for him. He left the Temple just after he heard that the disciples would be flogged."

"What! He's left the faith?"

Stephen raised his hand. "Oh, no, it's nothing like that. When Dorian saw the disciples' courage today, he decided to go home with the hope that he might lead his grandfather to the Lord."

Nathan clenched tight fists. "Lord, go before him!"

"Your faith grows fast!" Stephen said with a smile.

"If only my own father would believe what I have seen and heard."

Stephen studied him with concern. "You know, I will pray for you if you decide to go talk with him. You're his son. I'm sure he misses you."

Nathan stood. "It won't be today," he confessed. "I need time to think. Time to pray."

Stephen rose to put his hands on Nathan's head. "May the Lord bless you and keep you." He spoke in their beautiful Hebrew tongue.

Nathan smiled. "I'm going outside for some air." He walked out into the city and wandered through the streets until the first gray shades of night filled Jerusalem.

9

THE LAST TRIP HOME

Alarge white chunk of moon lighted Nathan's way the night he risked going home. When he walked through his own garden gate, he felt he had entered a world that was at the same time strange and familiar in the sharp moonlight. Silently he stood among the shadows near the wall. He wondered what Bena and Shem were doing now. He wondered and he waited until he saw his father climb the stairs to the open-air room on the roof. Whispering a prayer for Jesus' peace to be upon him, Nathan made his own feet go up the steps.

Softly he walked across the hard clay. Pale moonlight played on his father's robe as the man stood looking out over Jerusalem with his back to Nathan.

"Father?"

The man turned. "Nathan . . . ? Nathan!" In a moment he was there to enfold Nathan in his arms. They stood in silence for a long time. Then his father led him to a bench beside the wall at the edge of the roof. They sat down side by side. Suddenly nervous, Nathan dropped his eyes.

He felt his father's arm around his shoulders. "You've come home," he said.

Nathan found the courage to look at him. His father's face seemed white in the moonlight. "I don't think so," he admitted. "I just came to say . . . I'm sorry for the pain I'm causing you."

"Nathan." His father spoke his name again. "Nathan. I want you to come home."

Nathan swallowed hard, knowing that his next words might cut him off from his father's love forever. "I've . . . become a follower of Jesus. Father—"

His father stood. He tore his robe. "Why? Why did you do this?"

Nathan wrung his hands. "I love you, Father . . . but I believe Jesus arose from the dead. I have heard it from the lips of the disciples who were flogged. . . ."

"Why do you believe them and turn your back on everything I taught you as a child?"

Nathan hesitated. "Because I see how much they sacrifice to keep saying that their Messiah is alive. . . . And I've seen miracles, and I've experienced their kindness—even through the weeks when I refused to believe. . . ."

His father's eyes were wet when he gently plucked the shoulder of Nathan's tunic. "They've fed and clothed you?" he asked.

Nathan nodded. "It's not what I have here, but it's

enough. In fact, I would feel happier now than ever before—if I had your blessing. . . ."

His father looked at the sky. "How can I give my blessing when you're walking away from everything I hold dear!"

Nathan hung his head, praying silently, *Lord, what do you want me to do?* He looked at his father again. "I want you to know that I do study the Scriptures every day. Sometimes they mean so much to me that Stephen and I stay up half the night reading them by the dim lamplight."

His father made no reply.

"I tell you this because I want you to know that I do love God and want to honor him. I have not walked away from that."

"What about the Temple? You don't come there anymore."

"At first it was because I was afraid I'd see you," Nathan answered slowly. "But now that I believe Jesus' death on the cross paid the price for my sin, I don't see the need for our altar or our sacrifices."

With his arms folded across his chest, Benjamin bar Azmon surveyed the dark city.

Nathan got up. "I know I hurt you with these words. But you asked me. You have taught me the importance of being honest and of living by the truth. I wanted you to know what I really feel."

His father shared a small, sad smile and a nod of his head. "You left this house saying that you weren't worthy to read God's Holy Word. You return saying that now you study it night and day. Something has changed inside of you, Nathan, but I'm not sure what it is."

Nathan risked a grin. "I've been thinking that I'm like that old man who had a shekel for you to weigh on the eve of the Feast of Harvest. His coin was lacking, and there was nothing the man could do because he didn't have another coin. But what a difference it would have made if someone had stepped right up to buy the sacrifice for him."

His father watched his eyes. "You're talking in a parable, son, and it's one I don't understand."

Nathan's voice tensed with emotion. "The law shows me, Father, that I cannot be good enough to stand before my God. My life, like that filed-down coin, is always lacking compared with God's perfection. But then Jesus came to Jerusalem. He substituted his life for mine. And since He was the perfect sacrifice, He paid the full price for my sins."

"Who gets you thinking such things?" his father asked, raising an eyebrow.

"The disciples—and Stephen. He's become my closest friend. We eat and pray together, and I go as often as I can to hear them teach in the streets."

"They are in the Temple, too," his father reminded him, "lecturing to anyone in the Court of Gentiles who will listen."

"Do you ever listen?" Nathan braved.

His father looked away. "Some Jewish leaders, such

as Nicodemus, now believe as you do. Do you know this?"

"Then don't you think there *is* a possibility that God has sent his Messiah in our lifetime?" Nathan asked, his spirit soaring.

"I will be as honest with you as you have been with me. At this point I don't know."

"Then come to hear Stephen speak on the Scriptures. Listen and ask him questions. He's in the Temple almost every day. See what you think of what he has to say."

"All right," his father answered. "I'll consider it at least."

Nathan's heart was pounding with excitement. He could have spoken all night about these things, but his father grew quiet. After a moment, he walked to the stairs. Nathan followed, not knowing what would happen next. They went down into the garden. A lamp burned in the niche of the house wall, and Nathan could clearly see his father's worried eyes.

"What will you do now?" his father asked.

Nathan shivered. He took it to mean that he was no longer welcomed under this roof. "I will do whatever you want," he said. "Go or stay as you desire."

His father smiled a little. "It's strange," he said. "The man inside you seems to have grown while you were away."

Nathan looked at him without understanding. His father sighed. "You know, more than anything I want my son to be a man who follows God."

"That is what I want to do, Father. My love for the Almighty One grows every day. I want to live for him."

His father's eyebrows raised. "If half the temple officers told me that right now, I would not believe a single one of them. They serve the Lord to serve themselves with wealth and comfort and prestige. But you? When you say your heart is turned toward God, I believe you."

A sudden breeze twisted the lamp flame. Nathan's father put a hand behind it and blew it out. "It's late. Come sleep in your own bed tonight," he offered. "Then tomorrow, do what you think the Lord wants you to do."

At dawn the next day Nathan slipped from his silk sheets and headed back to Stephen. He found his friend repairing a leaky roof for an old man named Keros.

"Well, gird up your loins," Stephen called out cheerfully when he saw him. "Climb up here. I could use a hand."

Nathan tucked the hem of his garment into his belt and scaled the wall. The brown grasses and weeds had already been pulled from the soft pockets of roofing clay. Stephen was mixing fresh mud to pack into weak spots of the otherwise rock-hard earthen cover. Together they filled the holes. Then Nathan leaned into the heavy stone roller that was used to flatten out and pack the new clay. Stephen finished the job for him.

They both took a short rest in the shade while the new roof dried. "Has Dorian returned?" Nathan asked anxiously.

"No," Stephen said. "I was hoping that we'd hear

from him by now." He changed the subject. "Tell me about your visit home."

Nathan drew his knees up to his chin. "I think Father will come hear you teach someday," he reported excitedly. "Even though he is very upset now, he did not forbid me to come back to you."

"Well, that's fine," Stephen said. "Let's check our work. Then I'll get ready to go to the Gentile court to speak this afternoon."

Nathan found that it was hard to keep his place in front of Stephen when he preached. Those with illnesses and deformities continually jostled and pushed him until they made their way to Stephen's feet. When suffering ones completely ringed him, Stephen paused in his wonderful explanation of Jewish Scriptures. He crouched down among the unlearned listeners. With his hands on their foreheads and cheeks, he spoke in simple words so that even they could understand the reason for Christ's coming to earth.

As he did this, the power of God drew down around them: blind men saw; wounds were healed; the lame walked. Miracles happened within reach of Nathan's hand. At the same moment his father stepped into the crowd.

To Stephen, Nathan knew, the amarkal and the beggar had equal standing, so he didn't even trouble his friend to point out his father's arrival.

Eventually Stephen straightened from his work.

Some Greek-speaking Jews called out to him. "Wise teacher, you want us to believe that the Temple is no longer important to Jews. Yet you yourself come here every day. Tell us clearly now: what *do* you believe?"

Stephen looked at the temple officials, including Nathan's father, who were watching him. Nathan knew that remarks against the Temple could land Stephen in prison. Silently he prayed that God would give Stephen a wise answer for these mockers.

"You are trying to lay a snare for me," Stephen said. "I know each of you by name, and I can see that if you truly were concerned about this place, you would be here every day as the temple Jews are." Some Levites nodded in agreement. "Instead you hold your meetings in your own synagogue. So when I am finished here, I will be glad to meet with you there."

The Greek-speakers did not give up. "You play with our words, Stephen. Talk to us as a man. We came to learn what your Christ said about the Temple. It is reported by Pharisees that he said 'One greater than the temple is here.' In saying this, was he not speaking of himself?"

Stephen looked them in the eye. "I will not deny it. But do you know that in the same breath he taught them the meaning of those words. Quoting from our prophet Hosea, he reminded them of God's own thoughts: 'I desire mercy, not sacrifice,' says the Lord."

The men threw up their hands. "See! See!" they shouted out to the temple officials. "He speaks against the temple sacrifices. Pressure him, and he'll say that the death of a criminal did away with sin."

Stephen raised his hands. "I speak for the work of Christ—"

But priests and Levites stepped toward him. "Keep silence, now," they warned. "This courtyard is no place for your defense. Your brothers in the faith accuse you of speaking against the Temple and God. We will take you before the Sanhedrin so that the council can settle the matter of whether or not you are a blasphemer." Guards were called. Roughly they grabbed Stephen's shoulders and tied his wrists together. Nathan, his heart beating wildly, pounded his fists into the rock-hard back of the nearest guard. "Don't take him!" he cried out. But the Levite didn't even look in his direction. Two of the guards walked away with Stephen trapped between them. Nathan crumpled to his knees in despair.

It was his father who pulled him up.

"I have seen what they do to the believers, Father," Nathan moaned. "I watched the floggings. And now, they're taking Stephen—"

"Nathan! Stephen needs you!" His father's voice broke through his angry tears. "Run. Get disciples who can speak for him. Bring everyone to the council as quickly as you can."

Nathan blinked at his father's urgent plea. "I will," he cried, already scrambling to his feet. He looked around the courtyard. Where were the believers? He moaned in desperation. Any other day they would be here. He plowed through the temple crowds and into the quieter streets.

His chest was heaving painfully when he finally found Peter and Andrew in the house of one of the believing Jews. "Waste no time," he panted. "Get to the Sanhedrin. Stephen is on trial."

Mindless with worry, he raced through the streets yelling out to anyone who might be in workshop or garden. "The council holds an innocent believer! Run there! Speak in favor of this man!"

Suddenly he was pushed against the wall. With blurred vision he recognized the familiar face of the old man Keros. He was using all his strength to hold him still.

"Nathan, Nathan," he said, "fear has set you wild. Be still. Let God speak to your troubled heart."

He rested just a moment. "You're right, Keros," he said. "But they've taken Stephen prisoner. Now let me go. I need to get back to the Temple."

Keros nodded and let him loose. Nathan walked one street and then ran the rest of the way.

As soon as he reached the Court of the Gentiles, it was clear that something was very wrong. A knot of angry priests, perhaps numbering close to a hundred, blocked the entryway to the council room. Nathan danced on his toes, trying to get a glimpse of what was taking place at the doorway. Hundreds more people gathered as he tried to see. Finally he risked his life by falling to his belly. Slowly he wove himself along the floor among a thousand pairs of moving feet.

At the doorframe of the council room he pulled himself up and was sickened by the sight before him. Like bees exploding from a hive, the leaders of the Sanhedrin were pushing out against the crowd that had come to wait for the outcome of Stephen's trial. With clubs and whips Levite guards started carving a path for the officials to move into the Gentile court. "Let them pass!" they shouted. "Let them pass!"

Then Nathan caught a glimpse of Stephen, being both dragged and pushed by the angry guards. Nathan threw out his hand, but the throng pushed on. He followed in its wake, unable to see Stephen anymore.

"Help him, Lord!" Nathan choked as he stumbled along in the suffocating storm of men who filled the air with sharp cries of "Blasphemer! Make him die!" In the frenzied crush, Nathan thought they all might perish for lack of air. But just when he felt himself fainting, the whole swarm of men squeezed through the outer gate. They burst into fresh air.

As Nathan took a breath, an ugly, triumphant shout rose from the leaders. Then a silence gripped the crowd. The dazed spectators fanned out to look down into a deep pit that lay against the city wall. Nathan glanced down too. Instantly he was dizzy with anger and pain.

At the bottom *Stephen lay sprawled across the dust.* His limbs twitched, then moved. He lifted his head. Pushed up his shoulders. Staggered to his feet. He raised trembling hands toward the sky. "Lord Jesus, receive my spirit!" he cried out.

"Stones! Stones!" the leaders on the wall yelled. Bricks and rocks appeared in every hand.

"NOOOOOOO!!!" Nathan screamed as the weapons found their mark.

Below them in the pit, Stephen reeled. The hurled objects pelted his head and chest and thighs. He dropped to his knees. "God," he pleaded, "do not hold this sin against them." Then slowly, like an old man dropping off to sleep, Stephen's head fell to one side. He collapsed in the dirt.

The ledge could not hold Nathan now. He threw himself down to find cracks in the stonework. His fingers dug at them as he pushed his feet over the wall. His toes scraped and found perilous footing. He lowered himself bit by bit, and then he took the long fall to the ground. He rolled, and in a moment he was with Stephen. He cradled the dead man's head against his breast. His sobs filled the air. He rocked and wailed, cutting himself off from any comfort offered by heaven or earth.

Only when his voice failed him did he realize that he was not alone. A few other believers had lowered themselves to the site of Stephen's stoning, and their tears and cries took up where his had finally died away.

Above them, Asher watched. "I warn you," he shouted. "Any man or woman who mourns this death or touches this body will be tried for this man's crime. Go away! Go away! It's the law. We must let the vultures clean his bones."

10

FLIGHT FROM JERUSALEM

But even under Asher's threats, three strong men cleared away the rocks that had pinned Stephen's legs. Women removed their head scarves to bind his loose limbs. Then with a count to coordinate the efforts from above and below, the believers lifted up the lifeless body and pulled it from the pit. They were on the wall again before Nathan realized that his own father bore the weight of Stephen's shoulders. He pushed his way to his father's side. Clutching Benjamin's soft robes, Nathan walked beside him to the place where women would prepare the body for burial.

When his father's grim task was done, Nathan took his arm. "How is it that you came to help him?" he asked.

"I heard his testimony in the council room," his father replied. "There is no doubt in my mind that God loved this man." He looked up, and Nathan watched the direction of his father's eyes. Asher had followed them.

Nathan's father started toward him, but the other

man waved his hands. "I want nothing to do with you, Benjamin," he said. "You have cast your lot with the believers. You have defiled yourself twice over by touching the body of this criminal."

"In the day of God's judgment, I choose to stand with this man instead of with you," Benjamin said bitterly. "Come to your senses, Asher. Can't you see that you are fighting against God?"

"You go with these poor, misguided people," Asher said with a pointed finger. "And I will make sure that everything you own comes to me."

"Take it," Benjamin said. "Look there—a young, strong, intelligent Jew lies dead. Why? Because he chose to believe God's promise and to speak for it. What comfort can our Temple bring if it is on the side of deaths like this?"

Asher laughed nervously. "By tomorrow you may come to *your* senses. But by then it may be too late. Even now the scholar Saul seeks permission from the council to search each house in the city for those who speak of Jesus."

"What does all this mean, Father?" Nathan asked fearfully, as Asher walked away.

"Only God knows," his father replied. "But one thing is already clear to me. This is my last day as an amarkal in the Temple of Jerusalem."

Toward evening that day, after Stephen's body had been buried, Nathan and Benjamin returned to their home.

"Go upstairs and gather the few things you need," his father told him. "We won't tell Shem and Bena what is happening unless we have to. I think it will be safer for them if they don't know."

Nathan went to his room. He rolled an extra tunic and a pair of sandals into his warmest cloak. Then he carried the small bundle to the door and placed it beside his father's.

Just as Nathan's father carried in a jar of water, Asher barged into their home. "Either you have taken up woman's work, Amarkal, or you are counting on a secret trip by night," Asher observed.

"This house may be yours when I leave," Benjamin warned him, "but only after I leave. Until then you are not welcome here."

"Welcome or not, I plan to stay—until Saul comes to question you."

"What!" Nathan cried. "You will go against your own flesh and blood to see us tried?"

"You two have gone against me," Asher responded with an angry shake of his head. "Everyone saw you mourning over Stephen. Now even my beliefs and intentions are held in suspicion."

"Well they should be," Nathan's father snapped.

Asher walked over and pushed Benjamin down onto the bench where he studied each day. "I have told the Sanhedrin that I will take custody of you until you confess in front of the man they are sending here."

"Why are you doing this?" his father asked. "I've already handed over to you every earthly thing I own."

"I need to prove my trustworthiness," Asher said. "I want Saul himself to know that I can be a friend."

His father groaned.

A knock pounded at the door.

"Already?" Asher sighed. "Nathan. Open it."

With weak hands Nathan pulled back the door. A bent old man stared into his face.

"Saul?" Nathan questioned.

The man ignored him. "The Amarkal Benjamin bar Azmon. Is he here? This is his house, isn't it?"

Asher came forward. He placed a hand on the door. "What is it? My brother cannot come to talk. He is busy preparing for an important guest."

The stranger scowled. "I'd say this was important enough," he fumed. "A short time ago my grandson left two perfectly matched doves in the hands of the amarkal's son. I expect the sacrifices have been well cared for, and I want them back. For this very day, they are needed in the worship of the Lord."

Nathan stopped breathing. *This man had to know Dorian. Surely this meeting had been planned.*

"I know about these birds, Uncle," Nathan said quickly, pinching the skin on his hand to keep his eagerness from giving him away. "They are just a little way down this street. Shall Father and I go now?"

"Benjamin and you?" Asher said. "Surely not." He began to close the door. "Go to the Temple, old man. Someone will help you there."

Instead of leaving, the stranger hobbled into the room. "Why, look, the amarkal himself," he said to Nathan's father. "Please, come quickly. The sun is going down. I must have this business done by nightfall. It will only take a moment of your time."

Nathan's father stood and looked warily at his brother. "What can I say?" he told the stranger. "My brother says I have pressing plans for the evening, but if it will only take a moment, Nathan and I will be glad to help you retrieve the sacrifice."

Asher stood powerless.

Nathan and his father walked from the room. As soon as they were outside, the old man pushed them into the bed of a two-wheeled cart hitched behind a nervous white horse. The old man had barely tumbled in with them before the driver of the little wagon jerked away. Asher saw what was happening. As the animal's hooves pounded the ground, he raced after them on foot. Nathan watched his angry uncle shrink behind them in the dust of their departure.

Patterns of light and dark shadows flicked across them as the cart careened through the narrow Jerusalem passageways. Before Nathan could comprehend it, they had burst through one of the city gates and dipped into the Kidron Valley. Nathan stared back at the wall of Jerusalem as they raced along the rough road to Bethany at only a slightly slower pace. Once the cart turned north of that town the horse was completely winded, and they slowed down.

For the first time the ride was steady enough for Nathan to lift his head above the sideboards. He saw their driver and leaped forward to throw his arms around

his neck. "Dorian!" he shouted. "I knew it was you all along."

"You could tell by my driving?" the boy teased with his dark eyes dancing.

Another moment, and Nathan's laughter dissolved into tears. "Our friend Stephen is dead," he said. "Perhaps you have not even heard."

Tears flowed from Dorian's eyes, too. "I know. Grandfather and I just came today to see him. We heard of his death. We learned of the danger you were in. So we got directions to your house and came up with this plan. The centurion who had been Stephen's friend gave us the mare and wagon."

"Bless you, Dorian," Nathan said, slapping him on the shoulders. "You saved our lives."

Both boys looked back to the odd sight that was behind them: a dignified amarkal and a wiry old man, their arms intertwined, rode in the bed of the cart.

Nathan shook his head. "I never in my life saw anything so wonderfully strange." He laughed.

"It's just as peculiar a sight from back here," the old man teased. "In front of us, there's this heathen boy and a Jew hugging each other like long-lost brothers raised under the same roof."

"Well, it feels like that just now, Grandfather," Dorian put in. "And why not? Don't we all have the same heavenly Father?"

Nathan looked to his father. The man was nodding. "We do, and blessed be his name, He remains true to a thousand generations of those who put their trust in him."

"So where to?" the old man said as he watched the sun sink into the road they had left behind. "Darkness will be on our side now. Hopefully we won't be followed."

Dorian encouraged the mare to quicken her pace. "How about Neapolis or Sebaste?" he suggested. "From what I've heard, other believers who plan to flee tonight will be heading north into Samaria."

"Wherever God leads," Nathan's father said excitedly. "It is a new day. Let us give it over to God."

Dorian drew the horse to a standstill, and the four of them pulled themselves together to commit their way to Christ.

Then in the purple twilight, they headed on.